## Praise for
## *Pass the Faith, Please*

"It is the greatest desire of every Christian parent to pass on a vibrant, living faith to our children. Lori's book is an honest, practical road map that puts flesh on good intentions. Enjoy the trip!"

> —SHEILA WALSH, author of *The Heartache No One Sees* and *A Love So Big*

"Lori Borgman reminds us all, with a dash of humor and a dollop of reality, that we are our child's best teacher. Children learn faith—like they learn manners—by our example and teaching. Busy moms everywhere will appreciate the candid treatment of the topic of passing on our faith."

> —VICKI CARUANA, America's Teacher™, author of *Giving Your Child the Excellence Edge*

"In the spirit of Erma Bombeck, Lori Borgman's *Pass the Faith, Please* entertains us with the joy and humor of family life that leaves every reader eager for another helping."

> —ELAYNE BENNETT, president and founder of the Best Friends Foundation

"A fresh vision for instilling faith through life's ordinary moments."

—SUSAN ALEXANDER YATES, coauthor (with John Yates)
of *Character Matters: Raising Kids with Values That Last*

"Lori Borgman demystifies the process of passing faith on to a child, making it a seamless part of the rituals of family life: mealtime, bedtime, chore time, and Sunday worship. Her writing style is fresh, frank, and fun."

—MARY BETH LAGERBORG, media manager of MOPS
International (Mothers of Preschoolers) and author
of *Once-a-Month Cooking*

"Once again, fellow Hoosier Lori Borgman uses her trademark blend of wit and wisdom to deliver an important message to the family. *Pass the Faith, Please* is an essential book for parents interested in passing on faith, character, and values to the next generation."

—CONGRESSMAN MIKE PENCE

# PASS *the* FAITH, *Please*

*Nourishing Your Child's Soul in the Everyday Moments of Life*

# Lori Borgman

WATERBROOK
PRESS

PASS THE FAITH, PLEASE
PUBLISHED BY WATERBROOK PRESS
2375 Telstar Drive, Suite 160
Colorado Springs, Colorado 80920
*A division of Random House, Inc.*

ISBN 1-57856-725-4

Library of Congress Cataloging-in-Publication Data
Borgman, Lori.
  Pass the faith, please : nourishing your child's soul in the everyday moments of life / Lori Borgman.—1st ed.
     p. cm.
  ISBN 1-57856-725-4
  1. Christian education—Home training.  I. Title.
BV1590.B67 2004
248.8'45—dc22

2003017826

Printed in the United States of America
2004

10 9 8 7 6 5 4 3 2

*To Mom and Dad*

# Contents

# Dear Parent

• • • • • • • • • • • • • • • • • • • • • • • • • •

This book is not a primer on theology. (For that, see John Calvin.) It is not a catechism guide. (See Martin Luther.) Nor is this book a step-by-step how-to manual. (See Martha Stewart.) It is simply one parent's reflections on valiant—and sometimes not so valiant—attempts to pass on key components of her faith to her children in the course of everyday life.

As parents, you and I have roughly eighteen years to imprint life's basic lessons onto the hearts of our children. Naturally, this includes a wide variety of things, from the need to put the milk back into the refrigerator when finished to the value of doing extra-credit assignments in school. Hopefully, some basic lessons on faith will be taught as well.

Eighteen years seems like a long time when you bring that little bundle home from the hospital. Older women whose children are grown may look at you with your ducklings in tow and say, "Enjoy them while they're little; the time passes quickly." If you're having one of those not-so-good days, you may think, *Well, lady, the time isn't passing quickly enough.* And then it happens. One day you blink twice, turn around, and your kids are *not* little anymore. They're shaving, shopping for prom dresses, driving a car, and making plans for a mission trip to Haiti. It seems like only yesterday you told them that under *no* circumstances were they allowed to leave the backyard.

Of all the lessons a parent teaches a child during those fleeting years of childhood, the most important are the lessons of faith. Without faith and a moral compass, what's the point? Without a core set of convictions and beliefs, an understanding of our heavenly Father, a faith you can hang your hat on during times of trial, it's all little more than chasing after the wind.

So what *are* the key components of faith? First on the list is a personal relationship with Christ. We want our kids to know Christ and to know what type of people He calls His followers to be. We want our children to know how to think intelligently from a biblical perspective. We want them to grasp the essence of loving God with their whole being and their whole life. We want them to have teachable spirits and a measure of humility. We hope they will develop a good work ethic that appreciates all tasks, be they big or small, extraordinary or menial, and that they will do all things with the intent of honoring God. We want them to be people of character who know the power of prayer and the satisfaction of putting the needs of others before their own. We want them to grasp the power of repentance and forgiveness. Forgiveness—boy, is that important. What family could survive together under one roof without forgiveness? Above all, we want them to have a dynamic, living faith; not a petri-dish clone of our faith, but their own faith—a rock-solid belief system that seamlessly weaves the natural with the supernatural, the physical with the metaphysical.

How does a parent do all that? How does a parent ascend to such lofty heights while tethered to piles of laundry, unpaid bills, and a yapping dog? Well, how did Christ teach that gaggle of twelve who were under His tutelage? He taught while they walked, while they prepared meals, while they ate, while they built fires, and while they drifted in a boat.

There's nothing dramatic about passing on the faith. Oh, sometimes there are fireworks or one of those rare but unforgettable on-the-road-to-Damascus experiences, but for the most part, it's a quiet action. Passing on the faith is a slow, steady process that happens day in and day out—while packing sack lunches, checking book bags, talking over milk and cookies, or matching the clean socks fresh from the dryer. A parent imparts the lessons of faith the same way Christ taught the Twelve: within the holiness of the mundane.

# Chapter 1

# Pull Up a Chair

*Now About Your Teaching Job*

● ● ● ● ● ● ● ● ● ● ● ● ● ● ● ● ● ● ● ● ● ● ●

Three teenage driving permits, five pounds, and four years ago, something strange began happening. When I spoke to groups of young mothers, women would come up to chat at the close of the event, but that wasn't unusual. What was unusual was that, invariably, at least one pretty gal in her mid-twenties or early thirties, with a diaper bag under one arm and a toddler under the other, would step forward and say, "Thank you. It's so good to hear the perspective of an older woman."

The first time it happened, I looked to my left and then to my right. I spun completely around and realized she was talking to me!

Older woman? *You talkin' to me, darlin'?* This gal had no idea how close she was to physical danger.

It hurt. It really did. I have never thought of myself as an older woman. I still don't. Old? I sing with the car radio. I dance with the mop and can still jump up on the kitchen counter when I need a bowl from a top shelf.

Some days I feel so young as to border on childlike. Those would be days when I'm at my parents' home in Kansas City. During my last visit there, they reminded me not to put silverware down the garbage disposal (whew, that was a close one!), to take quarters to the car wash (aren't those the big silver ones with the eagle on them?), to be careful of the lid on a newly opened can (you can get CUT!), and not to lose the house key (so much for my dropping it off at the federal prison in Leavenworth).

Since moving out of their house, I have married and maintained a family and home for twenty-four years. I have learned to distinguish between termites and carpenter ants, three times I have rolled through the doors at the hospital marked "Delivery," and I write a nationally distributed newspaper column—but in my mother's and father's minds, I will always be age ten.

Then again, maybe I do qualify as an older woman. I was out for lunch with a group of friends when a snicker started around the table. One of them claimed the waiter had addressed me as "Miss." I didn't hear it, yet my friends—all but one of them younger than me, nonetheless fine and decent people—found the event a source of sidesplitting amusement.

Then there was that unpleasant situation with the eye doctor's office. I had phoned to schedule an appointment for an eye exam. The voice on the other end of the line was chipper, upbeat, and bubbly, as only a dewy, twenty-something female can be.

We agreed on an appointment time, and then she asked for some new-patient information.

"Name?" she cheerfully requested.

I gave her my name and heard her fingers clicking rapidly on the keyboard. *Clickety-clickety-clickety-clack.*

"Address?" she chirped.

I gave her my address and again heard her fingers clicking rapidly on the keyboard. *Clickety-clickety-clack.*

"Date of birth, by month, day, and year, please," she said.

"Ten, six, fifty-four," I replied.

*Click, click,* pause…

"Would that be NINETEEN fifty-four?" she asked.

"No, honey, EIGHTEEN fifty-four. I used to play marbles with Abe Lincoln's kids!"

I didn't really say that, but I felt like it. Which is actually another sign of aging—being blunt with strangers.

I choose to think that the younger women who thank me for the perspective of an older woman are talking about experience. They have toddlers in tow; I have three teens. They're serving macaroni and cheese for dinner; we've graduated to pork chops and serrated knives.

Chronologically I may not be old, but in mother years I have been around the block a few times. I've been around it with a baby stroller and with a toddler seat on the back of my bicycle. I've been around the block chasing a pink Big Wheel and steadying a kid on a little Huffy bicycle with wobbly training wheels. I've been around the block sprinting sack lunches to the bus stop, and I've white-knuckled my way around the subdivision more times than I care to count teaching teens to drive.

I'd never given pen-and-paper deliberation to the particulars of what parents teach children, and how we pass on the faith, until one day the phone rang and a voice on the other end asked if I would participate in a daylong seminar with a lineup of other speakers. This man wanted me to do a workshop on how parents can pass the baton of belief from one generation to the next.

"I bet you'd like the perspective of an older woman," I said.

"How did you know?" he asked.

"Lucky guess."

What an assignment. And what an assignment dear to my heart. We live in a culture where children have become the equivalent of designer throw pillows—trendy decorator accessories. Children have become mini-adults we dress up for holidays and special occasions and parade for display. And if they're not accessories, just listen to some parents and you'll learn that they're something else—a drag. They're a burden. Kids are an irritating interruption in the very busy and important schedules of adult lives. It's a shameful attitude. In the words of Perry Mason and Ben Matlock, I'd like to say, "I object."

## Precious Gifts

For starters, children are not a burden. How can I be so sure?

Jesus didn't display anger very often, but one of the few times He did was when the disciples tried to keep children from Him. Jesus loved children. Children are dear to the heart of Christ. It follows that if children are dear to the heart of God, then they should be dear to this human heart of mine.

Children truly are a gift.

I wish I could say that thought was original with me, but it's not. Actually, it comes from the psalmist, who wrote, "Behold, children are a gift of the LORD" (Psalm 127:3).

Now I don't know how many children the psalmist had. I don't know whether he had toddlers or preschoolers or teenagers when he wrote that verse. I don't even know if his kids were loud and rambunctious, forever hauling home poisonous snakes, or if they were quiet and demure, content to collect shells and draw pictures in the sand. Who knows; maybe he penned that thought while sipping a cup of coffee the morning after his ninth and last child rolled up his mat, slung his camelhair jacket over his back, and struck out on his own. What I do know is, despite the passing of time, that statement still rings true today. Children are a gift.

Just ask the 6.5 million couples struggling with infertility. Thousands of them so deeply believe children are a gift that they gladly cross twelve time zones and shell out dollar bills in extremely large denominations for the opportunity to adopt a baby from Russia or China. Ask the determined folks who fight to rescue children from the red tape of foster care. Or ask the medical personnel with broken hearts and tear-stained cheeks, the ones who treat children with cigarette burns and bruises up and down their spines.

Yes, children are a gift. Yes, *your* children and *my* children.

That toddler who just ate potting soil from a bag in the garage and shoved a pink hair bow into the VCR? A gift!

That six-year-old with the dirty neck, ladybugs in his pocket, and Hawaiian Punch stains all over his T-shirt—the same one who tried to swipe a pack of gum when your back was turned in the checkout aisle? Yes, he's a gift.

That middle-school child who comes out of her room only to shower and recharge the portable phone? That's right, she's a gift.

That teenage girl having a bad hair day, talking on the sassy side, pushing your button about a movie *all* the other kids get to see? A gift.

And what about that special-needs child with muscular dystrophy, spina bifida, hearing loss, or failing vision? How about the developmentally delayed child or the young diabetic or the little tyke with a neurological disease that has no name? Gifts, each and every one of them.

Your children, my children, they are all a gift. True, some days they are a gift we'd like to return, but nonetheless they are a gift.

Granted, some gifts arrive looking more lovable than others. Some arrive like a velvet box from Tiffany's, wrapped with a comely satin bow. Others debut looking like a refugee from a white-elephant grab bag. Personalities clash. Sparks fly. Patience wears thin, and you wonder if Somebody Upstairs wasn't exactly clear on your size and fit.

Then one day, regardless of shape, size, or packaging, do you know what those gifts do? They silently weasel into your heart and lay claim to prime real estate. Signed, sealed, delivered. Smart parents learn that a child is the most precious gift of all.

But as I was saying, our culture doesn't always share the view that children are a gift. A few months after my first book came out, a producer of one of the national television talk shows phoned to interview me as a possible guest. She had several questions she wanted to ask. The first one was if I had a terrible birth story that I would like to share with viewers. She wanted something graphic and memorable. "You know, some story about giving birth that was pretty awful," she said.

I told her that nothing with a lot of screaming and hemorrhaging came to mind, but I would think on it. The producer was sweet about it and said, "Okay, girl, that's fine."

She continued, "I noticed in your bio that you have *threeeeee* teenagers. Wow! How do you make yourself get out of bed in the morning? Three teens? That must be your worst nightmare come true."

I considered her comment and said, "You know, opening my front door and seeing Charles Manson on the other side would be my worst nightmare come true. But my kids? No."

## Our Primary Responsibility

Children truly are a gift. Having the gift of a child is a tremendous privilege. And, of course, with privilege comes responsibility.

Bill Bennett, renowned author and former secretary of education in the Reagan administration, has a saying that I love: "Not every teacher is a parent, but every parent is a teacher." He's right on the money. Parents are the primary teachers, and our homes function like little one-room schoolhouses.

In the home children learn the fundamentals of relationships, friendships, and marriage. Around the kitchen table, during bedtime rituals, and seated with the family at worship services, children learn the building blocks of prayer and faith. In the home, in the family room, in the backyard, or on the front porch, children learn character traits such as honesty, integrity, loyalty, and diligence. In the home children learn the greatest commandment: "Love the Lord your God with all your heart, and with all your soul, and with all your mind" (Matthew 22:37). In ordinary homes built of wood and glass and brick and stone, children learn the value of knowledge, gain an appreciation for God's awesome creation, and savor the satisfaction of pleasing God by serving others.

Most of us send our children to public or private schools. Professional teachers, coaches, and music instructors help teach our children, but every child's primary education should be rooted and grounded in the home. Parents bear the primary responsibility for a child's mental, emotional, and spiritual development—not the school, not the day care, not the baby-sitter, not the church, and not Aunt Tillie.

Why is a parent such a natural and influential teacher?

Parents are powerful teachers because nobody loves a child like a parent. Mind you, it's not that the rest of the world doesn't find your child positively adorable. It's just that nobody beams with love and warmth for a child the way a mom and dad do. Nobody busts buttons with pride the way a father does, and nobody has invested sweat, tears, and stretch marks in a child the way a mother has.

In most cases—and, sadly, there are exceptions—*nobody* loves a child like a parent. If you have ever helped in a preschool or a kindergarten or worked in the church nursery, tell me you didn't hesitate a whole lot longer to wipe that big, wiggly green thing out from under the nose of someone else's kid than you did with your own. You bet you did! Nobody loves like a mom. Nobody loves like a dad.

Yet a growing number of parents don't want to be bothered with the responsibility of teaching their children. I marvel at the parents who bail out when the teaching gets tough and put their kids on autopilot.

We wouldn't put the family bill-paying system on autopilot. "Oh, the finances will take care of themselves. I think I'll just leave the phone bill, the gas bill, the Visa bill, and the car insurance premium heaped in a pile. When they think the time is right, they can write themselves checks for the correct amount and find their way to the mailbox."

What happens when you put dinner on autopilot? I've yet to see potatoes jump out of the refrigerator, peel themselves, hop into a kettle of boiling water, mash themselves, hook up with a nice meatloaf and a tossed salad, and make their way to the table. Adult lives crumble when we run them on autopilot, but somehow we think the children will be just fine.

Teaching a child is a parent's primary responsibility. The Bible is adamant on this score: "Train up a child in the way he should go, even when he is old he will not depart from it" (Proverbs 22:6).

## The Ways We Teach

So exactly *how* do we teach our kids? Through stories. Through mealtime prayers. On the sidelines at soccer games, raking leaves in the backyard, or just hanging out on a Sunday afternoon.

This style of teaching has been around a long time. In Deuteronomy we read,

> These commandments that I give you today are to be
> upon your hearts. Impress them on your children. Talk
> about them when you sit at home and when you walk
> along the road, when you lie down and when you get up.
> Tie them as symbols on your hands and bind them on
> your foreheads. Write them on the doorframes of your
> houses and on your gates. (Deuteronomy 6:6-9, NIV)

Catch all the verbs in that passage? There's a lot of action, movement, and energy on the part of the parent—*impress* these words, *talk* about these words, *write* these words. The teaching sounds as constant and natural as breathing. In and out, in and out. Teaching is to become such a natural part of everyday family life that sometimes we'll forget we're doing it. Inhale, exhale. Inhale, exhale. Thaw the roast, fold the white clothes. Inhale, exhale.

Sometimes we teach methodically and deliberately, with careful consideration. Other times we teach by accident and with spontaneous candor, like when my then six-year-old son looked up from the breakfast table one morning and said, "Mom, what's sex?"

I launched into an explanation starting with the birds and the bees. I'd worked my way through the difference in plumage between the male cardinal and the female cardinal when he interrupted, saying, "Oh, well, the form on the cereal box says, 'Sex. Check male or female.'"

We teach on family vacations and on the way to Grandma's house for Thanksgiving. We teach as we take a meal to a family celebrating the arrival of a new baby, and we teach through the death of a family pet or the theft of a bike. We teach by talking, by laughing, in whispers, and in shouts. We teach through quiet bedside conversations or with excited voices while passing hot serving dishes around the dinner table. We teach on an evening stroll, gazing at a full moon. We teach in the car as we barrel down the interstate at seventy miles per hour under the noonday sun.

Deep down inside, we all know the primary way a parent

teaches. The point was driven home to me in a graphic way several years ago. Our youngest daughter, then age ten, had purchased a new wallet.

She took the wallet to Grandma's house, whipped it out, and began displaying its many fine features. She proudly displayed her new identification card, pictures of her school chums tucked into the plastic sleeves, and fifty-nine cents change in the coin compartment. She opened the fold where she would keep paper money, if she had any, and promptly pulled out a stack of cash register receipts.

She had a receipt from the neighborhood drug store for Jolly Ranchers, a receipt from a restaurant where the two of us had eaten lunch together three months prior, and an eighteen-inch-long receipt from Wal-Mart for toilet paper, shampoo, toothpaste, laundry soap, light bulbs, and glass cleaner. She had receipts from clothing stores, hardware stores, fast-food joints, video stores, and the post office.

I looked at my child and thought what any mother would think: *This child needs professional help! Why in the world would she save a huge bundle of receipts in her wallet?*

Then it hit me—she saved receipts because I save receipts. Routinely, after purchasing any item that has a likelihood of self-destructing or not living up to the warranty, I tuck the receipt into my wallet.

Here's the real killer. I had never once *told* this child to save receipts. I had told her to brush her teeth and hang up her clothes and pull the shower curtain inside the tub before she turned on the water. I had told her to capitalize proper nouns and ride her bike on the right side of the street, but not once had I told her to save receipts. Not a word spoken. I had never told her, but I had taught her.

That's exactly how we teach, which means we can't teach if we haven't learned the material ourselves. We become effective teachers when we make sure that our own hearts are in order, motivated in equal parts by a desire to please God and by the fear of little eyes watching us 'round the clock.

## A Call to Action (and Dinner)

I thought back to the caller seeking an "older woman" to present a workshop on passing on the faith. As I processed a mental outline of my presentation, I realized it was taking on the shape of a real snoozer. I'd be talking to moms—new moms weary from being up in the middle of the night with infants, women sapped from chasing toddlers, and middle-aged women windblown from the backdraft of the emotional roller coaster of their teens. For many it would be all they could do to escape for a few hours and hustle themselves to the conference. The last thing they needed was a dry, thirty-six-point presentation complete with overheads. They needed something memorable. Something visual. But exactly what, I didn't know.

I meandered out to the kitchen to rustle up dinner. As I began setting the table, it came to me. The key concepts of faith that kept running through my head lent themselves to a visual metaphor of having dinner together. Dinner is the time when, as a family, we gather to talk about the day's events, discuss what is happening in the world, compare schedules, air frustrations, and share laughs. My favorite time of day is after the meal when the entire family is home and everybody lingers long after the food has disappeared. The sky grows dark and the food hardens on the plates and the talking goes on and on. It's through all that conversation and loitering around the table that a lot of teaching transpires. Biblical truths become real-life applications. Abstract concepts travel from the head to the heart. Worldviews begin to take shape.

I pulled place mats out of the cupboard drawer and realized that even the table setting has some parallels to passing on our faith. Place mats, the foundation of every place setting, are like God's Word, the foundation of faith. The plates—which my children usually set, sometimes with good attitudes, sometimes with not-so-good attitudes—represent doing all things as unto the Lord. The napkins, quite naturally, represent forgiveness, and the knives and forks remind us to cut life's challenges into bite-size pieces and trust God for the outcome. The cups we drink from represent the cup of humility (I'll explain this later in chapter 8), which emphasizes learning the importance of a teachable spirit. All the metaphor needed was a sprig of parsley and love on the menu. Oh yes, and a couple of after-dinner mints—perspective and perseverance.

If you're intrigued by the idea of every parent being a teacher, if the thought of being the person most responsible for passing the baton of faith to the next generation makes you alternately smile and shudder, come on out to the kitchen, won't you? Pull up a chair and let's chat.

Regular or decaf?

# Chapter 2

# The
# Place Mat's Job

*Setting a Strong Foundation*

● ● ● ● ● ● ● ● ● ● ● ● ● ● ● ● ● ● ● ● ● ● ● ● ●

Every mother performs megatasks. They aren't megatasks in the sense that they are great tasks. They are mega in the sense that a mother does them a great number of times. As I set place mats around the table, I often wonder how many thousands of times I've gone through this routine. If I had a nickel for every time I laid down a place mat, I'd be so rich that I'd be Bill Gates. Yes, I'd be Bill Gates, and Bill Gates would be me— wandering around the kitchen at 5:30 at night with a pack of frozen chicken breasts clutched to his chest, wondering whether to accent with pasta or rice.

In any case, the reason we use place mats is simple. We have a nice oak table, and I wish it to live a long and happy life.

The place mat's job is to protect the table. Place mats form the foundation for every table setting at every meal.

In a similar way, God's Word forms the foundation of faith: "So then faith cometh by hearing, and hearing by the word of God," Paul wrote (Romans 10:17, KJV). As I lay place mats down time and time again to protect the table, in a similar fashion, God's Word must be laid down time and time again to protect a child's heart.

## Understanding Their Legacy

When God's Word is infused into a child's heart, that child not only learns Judeo-Christian principles of living but also gains a sense of place in time and history. He or she catches a glimpse of the big picture. Family history takes on a new dimension when young people realize that the God they worship is not some entity peculiar to the twenty-first century and the WWJD bracelet phenomenon. He was also the God of Abraham, Isaac, and Jacob. All of a sudden they realize they have something in common with Adam and Eve. Wow! And they thought Mom and Dad were old. The family tree goes way beyond Mom's branch in Missouri and Dad's offshoots in Ohio. It's pure revelation when they comprehend that we share the bloodline of all humanity. The fatherhood of God and the brotherhood of man take on deeper significance.

Consequently, as we trace our family tree back, we also discover that we share a rebellious streak that predates baby boomers and Woodstock. One day children grow to understand that they, too, given the opportunity, would have snacked on forbidden fruit in paradise.

By listening to Bible stories and reading the Scriptures, children come to know stories of faith, courage, victory, and suffering. Not only do they gain the advantage of learning from other people's mistakes, but they benefit from others' successes.

They need to know of Joseph, his beautiful tunic, and his jealous brothers, and how God can bring good out of evil. They need to know of Noah and the ark, of the young shepherd who became Israel's warrior and king, of Solomon's wisdom and riches, and of Moses' leading God's people through the Red Sea. Children need a foundation shaped by the poetry of Psalms, the wisdom of Proverbs, the bravery of Esther, and the boldness of the prophets. God's Word provides more than a foundation; it's part of the treasure chest of their inheritance.

What jewels our children will ponder in their hearts when they hear how Christ stood culture on its head, bestowing respect and regard on women and children, two of the most oppressed classes of His day. The miracles, the healings, the fruit of the Spirit, the Beatitudes, and the Sermon on the Mount will shape our children's thoughts for years to come. The journeys of the disciples, the Crucifixion and the Resurrection, the great chapter on love (1 Corinthians 13), and the discourse on law and freedom in Romans, hopefully, will all meld together to form a sure and solid Christian worldview.

## Shaping Decisions

The lessons a child can learn through Scripture go beyond recounting historical events and highlighting memorable characters. Scripture can teach children basic logic and reasoning. A serious student can learn some basics of debate, including how to structure an argument.

Linger in Psalms and Proverbs, and you can even develop an ear for the rhythm of language. Wade through the Books of the Law, and you gain an appreciation for detail and precision. The book of Numbers alone can give you a new respect for bean counters.

A love for God's written Word also cultivates a love for truth. I hope our children will discern the fingerprint of God whenever they encounter truth. God's Word is all truth, but no book can hold all of God's truth. The truths of physics and calculus aren't in the New Testament. The truths about electricity and color theory or about the mating habits of wolves aren't in the Old Testament, but they are nonetheless among the many truths that comprise God's universe. I want our children to recognize truth, whether it is found in the pages of a *New International* Bible or in a PowerPoint presentation in a botany class at a secular university.

As the knowledge of God's Word grows, so grows the foundation of faith. For some, God's Word may flow gently off the pages, silently and seamlessly forming a foundation. For others, the power of God may boldly lunge from the pages of Scripture, igniting a moment of turning to Christ, a specific point in time when the cornerstone of faith was first set in place. Regardless of whether the foundation begins to take shape gradually or quickly, the knowledge and understanding of Scripture is like wet cement that sets, cures, and eventually forms a solid base. In addition to providing a base for faith, the Bible provides a base for thought. This foundation helps a child frame a moral outlook that is pivotal in decision making and choosing between right and wrong.

The foundation of faith and thought profoundly influences the way children treat their friends and family. And one day down the line, when they become adults, that foundation of faith and thought will shape lifestyle decisions regarding how they live, what types of work they pursue, what types of citizens they are, how they handle a paycheck, and whom they choose to marry. Faith will determine whether they believe Christianity is something to carry with them into the schools, the workplace, and the marketplace, or whether it is something that's private, best left to that small window of time early Sunday morning.

## Building Confidence

A strong foundation of faith can also impart confidence. Genuine self-esteem is a result of understanding that every human being's true worth and value come from being made in the image of God. I can't give myself worth. A job, a career, a business, and a stock portfolio don't give a person worth. Children can't give themselves worth. None of us can earn worth or accrue value. Our fundamental worth as human beings comes from being made by and in the image of God.

In today's times children desperately need to know about genuine self-esteem, not the self-worship and narcissism the schools have been teaching: "I'm wonderful, I'm marvelous, I'm fantastic; therefore, I deserve." Or "I'm beautiful, athletic, or in the gifted program; ergo, I'm special."

Most of us just naturally esteem ourselves, think about ourselves, and obsess over ourselves. This tendency is also what makes us extremely boorish. Children (adults, too) are better off learning authentic self-esteem.

Authentic self-esteem comes from knowing what God says

about our true selves, warts and all. Self-esteem, security, and confidence come from understanding that the Creator knows every aspect of our being:

> O LORD, You have searched me and known me.
> You know when I sit down and when I rise up;
> You understand my thought from afar.
> You scrutinize my path and my lying down,
> And are intimately acquainted with all my ways....
> For You formed my inward parts;
> You wove me in my mother's womb.
> I will give thanks to You, for I am fearfully and wonder-
>     fully made;
> Wonderful are Your works,
> And my soul knows it very well.
> My frame was not hidden from You,
> When I was made in secret,
> And skillfully wrought in the depths of the earth;
> Your eyes have seen my unformed substance;
> And in Your book were all written
> The days that were ordained for me,
> When as yet there was not one of them.
> How precious also are Your thoughts to me, O God!
> How vast is the sum of them! (Psalm 139:1-3,13-17)

Now *that's* a confidence builder. As other stories and teachings of the Bible are told and retold, read and reread, time and time again, day after day, children will grow in their understanding of who God is and how much He loves them.

## As Your Child Grows

Our opportunities to teach and lay this critical foundation change as a child grows. When children are young, the window of opportunity is open wide. Little children love stories. Every child should have a basket or shelf full of favorite storybooks, picture books, and a beginning Bible. Nap time, bedtime, and hanging-out time are all perfect for introducing Bible stories of Christ's love and God's provision. Young children are a warm and receptive audience. They are also suspended in that golden age where they believe everything an adult has to say. Enjoy. It doesn't last long.

About the time children enter school, they begin thinking more logically. They often see things in black and white. That's nothing to be alarmed about; it's developmentally appropriate. They're at the age when they form a moral framework, when they begin to determine what is ultimately good and true. Sometimes this stage can be a little scary or even embarrassing, particularly when they blurt out that somebody "told a big ol' lie" or "That lady is not nice!"

You begin thinking, *Great! Now what have I done? I read the kid so many Bible stories, he's turned into a Pharisee!* Not quite.

The black-and-white stage doesn't last forever. Before you know it, they're midway through childhood, headed into the middle-school years and noticing shades of gray. Somewhere between the ages of eleven and thirteen, children become aware that there are layers and complexities to a decision or a choice. Things are not always a simple black and white. Sometimes there are shades of gray—steel gray, charcoal gray. They realize that things may not always be what they seem. They notice that people's words don't always match their actions, and their own actions don't always measure up to their words. In a nutshell, children become aware of ambiguity.

On the upside of this phase, children are now able to comprehend abstract concepts. On the downside, they can spot hypocrisy through walls and around corners. The real kick is they usually notice it in you, the parent. We would call this ashen gray.

This is the time to address the shades of gray that lie between the black and white. This is the time to teach about mercy and compassion, forgiveness, and new starts, and about how to help someone who is suffering the consequences of poor choices. This is the time to address loving the sinner but hating the sin.

Adolescence also marks the time when the window of opportunity for a parent's input begins to close. The window is not open nearly as wide as it once was. I've yet to meet the fourteen-year-old crying late at night, "Sit on my bed and read me another story, Mom. Please! Please!" Teaching at this juncture sometimes works better in terms of family reading, discussing books, magazines, movies, or popular music. An appetite for faith is more likely to remain strong when you keep age-appropriate resources available.

## Using Age-Appropriate Resources and Methods

When our middle child was about nine years old, she received her first "big girl" Bible. One morning I had slipped down to the family room a little after 6 A.M. for a few minutes of quiet before the rest of the troops rallied. I had a practice of sitting in a wingback chair with just one lamp on. (Let me be honest by noting that this is a ritual I have tried to cultivate on a daily basis over the years with mixed success.) On this particular day, with the rest of the house still dark and quiet, these few moments alone provided needed fuel for the action to come. I'd been reading for about five minutes when I heard footsteps padding down the stairs.

Clothed in her pajamas, a small form emerged from the dark, with her arms wrapped around her big girl Bible, and said, "I knew you were down here. I want to read with you."

It was one of those simultaneously shocking and golden

moments of parenting when you see that something you're doing might actually be taking hold.

"What are you reading? Let's read together," she whispered. Small snag. I was reading through the Bible that year and on that particular day I was in the book of Solomon. It had to be the raciest chunk of the Bible.

> To me, my darling, you are like
> My mare among the chariots of Pharaoh.
> Your cheeks are lovely with ornaments,
> Your neck with strings of beads.
> We will make for you ornaments of gold
> With beads of silver.
>
> While the king was at his table,
> My perfume gave forth its fragrance.
> My beloved is to me a pouch of myrrh
> Which lies all night between my breasts.
> My beloved is to me a cluster of henna blossoms....
> How handsome you are, my beloved,
> And so pleasant!
> Indeed, our couch is luxuriant! (Song of Solomon
>     1:9-14,16)

And now my little girl wanted to join me.

"Why don't we read in Mark?" I said. We read together. She joined me a time or two after that, and then she began reading on her own.

We did something similar with our son when he was in upper elementary and began losing interest in reading in general. He wanted to be doing a million other things that didn't involve books, and it showed. Considering his age, there was nothing terribly abnormal about that. Then one week at church I encountered a friend who had a copy of a comic-strip Bible. Old and New Testaments were told in full-color comic strips with action figures and cartoon dialogue. Noah had a brown robe, Moses wore hot pink, and David sported royal purple. The disciples frequently changed clothes, sometimes wearing solids, sometimes stripes, and the Virgin Mary had flowing, light brown hair. Storms were portrayed with dark ominous clouds and zigzag lightning bolts. It was just one "pow" and two "zaps" away from Batman. I remember thinking to myself, *What a gimmick. Whose bright idea was that?*

Well, guess who went out and bought a comic-strip Bible a few weeks later? It wasn't a case of dumbing down the Bible; it was a case of meeting a kid where he lived.

A parent can provide wonderful resources, but ultimately the decision to nurture a spiritual life has to come from within. One winter morning when our son was in high school, I noticed his light on under his door. He had been reading the

Bible on his own, privately but faithfully. (This time it was a study Bible for teens—the comic-strip Bible, while it had served its purpose, was short-lived.) That summer before our son's senior year in high school, I noticed some of our C. S. Lewis books had disappeared from the bookshelf. He'd been reading those as well. The next year Philip Yancey's books were in hot demand. Whether your children are preschool age or into full-blown adolescence, keep the resources available; you never know when interest will spark.

By the time kids hit high school, the window of opportunity for input is waiting to slam shut on your fingers. Oh, don't look so sad. By no means does this mean you're finished teaching. If you input the data when the window was open wide, now is the time for helping with access and application. In a courtroom this technique is called leading the witness, and it is generally unacceptable. In the classroom it's known as the Socratic method, and it is extremely popular. In parenting it's the only way to go.

With a shift in your approach, you now teach about God's Word by drawing out concepts and applying them to real-life situations. As I mentioned before, many of our best teaching times have been at mealtimes around the table. There's nothing like lingering after a meal, leisurely discussing current events, hot topics, and what's happening in your children's lives, in light of scriptural principles. The newspaper works as a natural launching point, as does the nightly news or what happened that day at school or on the job.

"What does the Bible have to say about dating?"

"What do you think Jesus would say constitutes a good education?"

"That's a nice paycheck you brought home. How do you think faith relates to wealth?"

"Environmentalists drove spikes into trees in an old-growth forest. The spikes could have injured or killed loggers. What do you think about that? Do you think God's Word gives us a mandate for how we treat the earth?"

"Does a pierced tongue fit with Paul's teaching on modesty?"

We never have a shortage of topics for conversation, but nonetheless we've also instituted the R&R activity: read and respond. I find something relevant, interesting, or thought pro-voking and leave it on the kitchen table with R&R written at the top. That means "read it so we can talk about it." The R&R response rate isn't always 100 percent, but it's close.

Once children hit their midteens, you're not giving direct input around the table, in the car, or while walking through the grocery store, but you're still teaching. You're helping organize stored data, pulling it from file folders and applying it to real life. You're helping young adults think as they maneuver through everyday life. Along with discussing, asking questions, and exchanging ideas, listen to your kids. Don't just listen to their obvious questions, listen to the question behind the question.

We all need to know why we're here, where we came from, who made us, and how we fit into the big picture. The answers, both broad and specific, are found in the pages from Genesis to Revelation. By teaching children and helping them apply biblical truth and principles to their everyday lives, we help them set the foundation of faith. The prophet Isaiah wrote, "The grass withers, the flower fades, but the word of our God stands forever" (Isaiah 40:8). You couldn't ask for a more solid foundation.

# Chapter 3

# "Wattsfirdinner?"

*Love in Generous Portions*

● ● ● ● ● ● ● ● ● ● ● ● ● ● ● ● ● ● ● ● ● ● ● ● ●

You know how some females naturally have the mothering gene? They instinctively know what to do for diaper rash, and they come hard-wired with fourteen lullabies. Well, I wasn't one of them.

When they told us in our childbirth classes that we would learn to distinguish a baby's different cries, and then hurriedly moved on to bathing a baby, I secretly panicked. Couldn't they give a few specifics? How about a chart? Maybe a sound bite or two? Would the wail for hunger be a different pitch than the wail for "change me"? Would there be a "whoop" at the end of a cry to signal boredom and "two whoops" to indicate pain?

Nobody else seemed concerned. Maybe I didn't have the instincts. Frankly, the thought of that teeny, tiny, helpless infant somewhat frightened me. Would I have what it took? Would I have enough love? Where was the love going to come from? How do you love a little preverbal creature who spends the bulk of all its waking hours exploding at both ends? Nobody seemed concerned about that either.

Then the baby came and the magic happened. Within days I was head over heels in love. He spit up on my shoulder, and I thought he was adorable. He blew out a diaper on my lap, and he was the most beautiful baby in the world. He followed the shadow of his hand on the wall, and I called Harvard. And yes, I learned to tell his tired cry from his ear-infection cry.

I loved him. And how! But the goo-gooing over him and cutting small locks of his hair and mailing them to faraway family members wasn't the heart of our love. In truth, both my husband and I had loved this child before we knew him. (That has a familiar ring, doesn't it?) We loved him in the womb before we knew whether he had ten fingers and ten toes, blond hair or brown. We loved him by making sure I took care of myself during my pregnancy and by arranging our finances and priorities so that I could leave my job to be home with him. We determined in advance to love him by preparing for him, by stocking needed supplies, and by a willingness to put some of our wants aside in order to provide him with a secure and nurturing home. At the heart of love is a commitment, even a duty, if you will.

So what was the fussing and squealing about when he smiled his first smile and made that first cooing sound? Those were the ribbons and lace wrapped around the heart of love. Those were the emotions swept high, the devotion intensified, and the sweetness of romance. When duty and devotion intertwine, it is sheer delight; but at the core, love is first a commitment. As C. S. Lewis wrote, "Christian love, either towards God or towards man, is an affair of the will."

## The Greatest Commandment

When asked what the greatest commandment is, Jesus replied, "'Love the Lord your God with all your heart and with all your soul and with all your mind.' This is the first and greatest commandment. And the second is like it: 'Love your neighbor as yourself'" (Matthew 22:37-39, NIV).

If love is an act of the will, and if a parent wills to love a child, the first place a child will learn about love is in the parent-child relationship. The first place the greatest commandment will be taught, and the second as well, is in your home. The most marvelous gift any parent can give a child is the gift of love. That commitment to love—at 2 A.M. when she spikes a fever, at 3 A.M. when the sheets need to be changed, and at 4 A.M. when she has set a distance record for projectile vomiting—is a fulfillment of duty, loyalty, and faithfulness that forms the basis of a child's first intimate relationship. That deep and permeating bond, created through the habits and rituals of daily routines, gradually paints a portrait of love. By witnessing the depth of a parent's love, children form deep and lasting impressions about the breadth and height of the Father's love.

You may have heard the story about Art Linkletter watching a small boy coloring wildly on a sheet of paper. "What are you drawing?" Linkletter asked.

"I'm drawing a picture of God," replied the little boy.

"You can't do that, because nobody knows what God looks like," Linkletter said.

"They will when I'm finished!" said the boy.

In spite of extremely high hopes, the little boy's drawing was not able to show what God looks like. However, in many ways, the love of a parent truly does show what God looks like. Granted, the picture of God painted by the love of a parent is incomplete and far from perfect, but hopefully the picture is several notches better than the little boy's wild scribbling.

God's pattern for parenting encompasses both love and sacrifice. God sacrificed His Son out of love. Christ sacrificed Himself in obedience to the Father. The Bible presents a clear pattern of putting ourselves aside in the interest of loving others. The message of love and sacrifice nearly shouts from the pages of the New Testament: The last will be first, and the first will be last! Greater love has no man than that he lay down his life for his friend! The greatest among you will be the least, and the least among you will be the greatest! If you want to find your life, lose your life! Love one another!

A home filled with Christian love will not be focused exclusively on the children or on the parents; it will be focused on one another. A home filled with God's love should be a place where all members willingly make sacrifices for one another—a husband for a wife, a wife for a husband, a child for a parent, and, yes, parents for their children.

## Lavish Love

First John 3:1 says, "How great is the love the Father has lavished on us" (NIV). *Lavish* means "to shower, deluge, heap, give, pour, and be generous with." The world interprets lavish love as a string of gifts: a new bicycle at five years of age, a shiny car at sixteen, and a trust fund at twenty-four. *Lavish* automatically conjures up images of boxes and bows, pretty trinkets, luxurious trips, expensive jewelry, and small appliances. (Well, you think of small appliances if you're a woman—big-screen televisions if you're a man.) Certainly there's an element of those things that is lavish, but more than anything they are indulgent. They address the outer-man (and believe me, there are times my outer-man does like to be addressed), but in the long run, a steady diet of materialism leaves the inner-man to languish in a state of insatiable greed and terminal boredom. This person is forever hungry but doesn't know what to cook.

The love the Father has lavished on us is a love that draws our hearts and turns our heads toward Him. The mercy and grace and forgiveness that come from the Father satisfy the soul and yield a deep and abiding peace. The Father's lavish love is lasting and life changing; the world's lavish love needs a lot of maintenance and extended-warranty agreements. In fact, most worldly love is far from lavish. It's stingy, conditional, temperamental, and self-centered. "I'll love—on my time, on my terms, at my convenience. How does Wednesday sound?" God's love does not revolve around convenience or materialism. The Father's lavish love is so powerful that it prompts receivers not to gain more for themselves, but to give. There's no getting away from the fact that love and sacrifice intermingle.

Where will a child witness such sacrificial love? In small acts of kindness such as putting down a magazine to help with a math problem or admire a ragweed bouquet. It happens when a parent turns off the television to give undivided attention. Sacrificial loves transpires when a dog-tired parent gets up off the couch and tends to a sibling skirmish because it's a teachable moment. Lavishing love on a child means having the fortitude to help shape character, to filter the steady flow of media filth that pollutes the home, and to do what needs to be done in the best interests of the family when you'd rather watch a ball game or take off with a girlfriend for coffee. Loving sacrifice happens when a father lays down his ego and sticks with a job he doesn't like because a family needs to put down roots. Loving sacrifice happens when a parent gives up a promotion that would require more travel and would disrupt family life.

Financial sacrifice is another expression of sacrificial love. With our level of affluence today, and a numbness to credit-card debt, this doesn't happen often, but it used to. A friend recalls thinking her mother had a strange attachment to a black cloth coat. The mother wore that coat year after year. The coat grew so old it hung like a rag. As a child, my friend thought her mother simply couldn't part with the black coat. Only as a young adult did she realize that her mother hung on to that old coat so her growing children might have the clothing they needed.

## When the Parts Become Stronger as a Whole

We live in a culture that exalts the love of self. Consumer magazines have gone from *Look* and *Life* to *People, Us,* and *Self.* Commercials blare: "You deserve a break today" and "L'Oreal—because you're worth it." Love of self has become a lucrative cash cow. We pride ourselves on rugged individualism and a fierce independence that owes no man. It's the American way. We foster an enduring sense of autonomy. While such notions can be rather romantic in a rustic Ernest Hemingway sort of way, they stand in direct contrast to Scripture. Believers are called to be interdependent, to be part of the body of Christ, where individuals come together to function as a whole, and, mysteriously, the whole becomes greater than the sum of the parts. Such is the love of a family; parts coming together, serving one another and growing stronger as a whole.

A child sees this model of love in the parent-child relationship and also in the husband-wife relationship. A marriage gives testimony to the mettle of love. Children can see how a dad and mom accommodate one another, please one another, and encourage one another. While children have the opportunity to observe a mother and father interacting during pleasant and uneventful times, they also have the opportunity to watch what happens during those not-so-good times. Every marriage has them. (It's okay to admit it. There's no such thing as a perfect marriage.) It is precisely in those trying times that children will see the strength of a covenant, a promise made before God. A child can learn, through your Frosty Queen snits and his I-can't-ever-do-anything-right soliloquies, that you love each other in spite of your imperfections and incredibly annoying quirks. They can see that our imperfections and shortcomings are what call us to Christ, the only love that is complete and the only love that never fails.

And what if you don't have a spouse? What if you are one of the thousands out there doing this parenting thing alone?

You're so exhausted that the thought of being vigilant about modeling the love of God is a touch more than your aching feet can bear. God knows about it. It's a tough row to hoe, but being a single parent and passing on the truths of the faith are entirely possible. Jesus said in Mark 10:27, "With people it is impossible, but not with God; for all things are possible with God."

I've never been a single parent, but with my husband's work schedule, there have been seasons when I sure thought I was. Second Corinthians 12:9 is a verse of great encouragement: "But he said to me, 'My grace is sufficient for you, for my power is made perfect in weakness'" (NIV). You can spend weeks running that verse through your mind when you're at your wit's end, putting the emphasis on different words. "*My* grace is sufficient for you." "My *grace* is sufficient for you." "My grace is *sufficient* for you." "My grace is sufficient for *you*." That reminder can take you through the chicken pox, a plumbing disaster, and two preschool conferences all in one day. It's a great reminder that we are up to the challenge.

With a single-mindedness, a commitment to love, and a determination to set priorities that strengthen the family, a single parent can model the love that is necessary. Your child may not be able to see the covenant love of a husband and wife in your home, but he or she can see it in their grandparents' relationship or in the marriage of an aunt or uncle or close family friends. When you're a single parent, training up a child is a goal within reach; you just have to throw a slightly wider net to pull in some extra help.

## Tending Fertile Ground

Transferring this concept of love—an act of the will, a mixture of duty and devotion, and the countercultural concept of selflessness—from hearth and home to the God of the heavens is another challenge. Loving the Lord your God with all your heart, all your mind, and all your soul is a tall order. A parent can model love for a child; marriage can model love for a child; a parent can encourage good habits, cultivate good character, discipline misbehavior, plant the seeds of virtue, and keep fertile soil around the heart. But, in truth, no parent can force a child to love God. You might achieve some temporary results by using force. But a strict and rigid conformity imposed from the outside often has a way of blowing up on the inside. While we may not be able to force love, we can certainly whet the appetite for love.

Theologian A. W. Tozer has said, "What comes into our minds when we think about God is the most important thing about us." As parents, this is the best place to start. Let your son know that the most important thing about him is not his ability to play sports or be the art student of the month. Let your daughter know that the most important thing about her is not her ability to excel at gymnastics or collect the most signatures in her yearbook. Let your children know that you believe the most important thing about them is invisible: the ability to love God with their heart, mind, and soul. Let them know it, and then live it yourself. As a general rule, what's important to you will become important to your child.

I remember driving along in the car with one of the girls behind me in a car seat, misbehaving. I don't remember what she was doing, but I do remember telling her to stop it. She answered in a little singsong voice, "But Mommy, I love you." Exasperated, I immediately shot back, "If you love me, you'll obey me!" It was true, but it struck me—how many times I had been the kid in the car trying to talk my way out of disobedience, saying, "But God, I love You." And God answers, "If you love Me, you'll obey Me."

A growing love for God, be it in the heart of a child or an adult, most naturally manifests itself in a desire to please God. The way we please God is to obey Him. "To obey is better than sacrifice" (1 Samuel 15:22). Obedience is the essence of loving God with heart, mind, and soul. When I think of obedience, I think of Mary who responded so graciously to the angel's shocking news: "Behold, the bondslave of the Lord; may it be done to me according to your word" (Luke 1:38). What a beautiful picture of loving God with heart, mind, and soul. What excitement must have filled Mary's home and heart that day.

Children gravitate toward excitement. While no parent can

force faith on a child, a parent's faith is able to generate a stirring and an energy that cause a child to ask, "What's all the buzz and how do I join the action?" It's important to emphasize the connection between love and obedience, but it's also important to nurture a zest for the Christian life that causes a small child to drag a chair over to the kitchen counter to get a better view of what's happening.

Create an environment where love is served in generous portions. Create a home atmosphere where belief is plausible. Cultivate an appreciation for God's creation and a tenderness for His people. Grow enthusiasm. Play hard. Get dirty. Serve freely. Leave the bland and tepid for the bored-with-life.

Loving the Lord your God with all your heart, mind, and soul and loving your neighbor as yourself provide a passionate focus for life. What more noble and worthwhile goal could there be than to love God with your whole person? It is an idea that turns the knobs on every door to the imagination. To love with every act of the heart, with every neuron in your brain, and with the whole of your soul is a breathtaking concept. This is not some lame platitude from a great teacher. It is not the tip of the week Dr. Phil regrettably left on the cutting-room floor. It's a directive from the lips of God. It's a command. Think boot camp. Think Marine Corps. *Semper fidelis.*

Fan the flame within your own heart, share the excitement, and pray that your children catch the fire.

# Chapter 4

# "Honey, I'm Home!"

*Establishing Rituals and Rhythm*

● ● ● ● ● ● ● ● ● ● ● ● ● ● ● ● ● ● ● ● ● ● ●

Whether or not they realize it, every family practices rituals, especially when someone leaves for the day or comes home. A kiss, a hug, or a "Have a good day" when someone leaves; a kiss, a hug, or a "How was your day?" when they return. When our kids were little, they got into this habit of hiding when my husband came home for dinner. They'd hear the garage door roll up and run to their hiding spots. They ran to the same spots day after day: beneath the table, next to the kitchen counter, and behind the sofa. He'd walk in and yell, "Honey, I'm home!" They'd jump out from their hiding places, screaming, "Boo!" and "Gotcha!" and then double over laughing as he feigned a terrible case of fright. Night after night they did this, and night after night he acted surprised. It was the prelude to every dinner. While other young families were setting the mood for dinner with candles or music, ours was jumping out from behind furniture yelling, "Boo!"

In what is either a testimony to the power of rituals or a frightening insight as to how insane this family truly is, that ritual is still in place. It doesn't matter if the kids who are home are in high school or college, when they hear that garage door roll up, they still think it's a kick to occasionally revert to that old shtick for a good laugh. What's more, whenever any of us comes home and walks through that door from the garage to the kitchen, we will yell, "Honey, I'm home." Maybe we do it out of habit because it was a ritual for so many years. Maybe we do it because it conjures up a wonderful memory filled with laughter and love. Maybe we just do it because we're a little wacky. In any case, it germinated with a simple ritual that began many years ago.

My husband and I have tried to create a variety of rituals to help pass on the faith to our children. Most of these rituals naturally took shape at three different times—dinnertime, bedtime, and Sunday mornings, or as the author of Deuteronomy would probably say, when we were by the table, lying down, or rising up.

## Dinnertime Rituals

The dinnertime rituals have changed as our children have grown and passed through different stages. When they were very little, we had one of those pottery jars that said "Promises" on it. I wrote verses on slips of paper and tucked them into the jar. The kids clamored over whose turn it would be at dinner to reach into the Promise jar, pull out a verse, and hand it to Mom or Dad to read. You would have thought it was a piñata loaded with Skittles. It made for a great frolic around the table and linked fun with learning. Once our children were able to read, they would take turns pulling a verse out of a little box we purchased at a Christian bookstore and reading it aloud themselves. They deemed it a high honor to be the chosen reader for even a short verse.

Once they were all nestled into elementary school, we would take turns reading from family-oriented devotional books. I know some families choose to be very structured about these things and would have readings every night. We operated rather casually, more on an as-needed basis. The flow of the week, as well as attitudes and events, clued us in as to when it was time to read a devotional together. We would also determine whether we had "learners" gathered around the dinner table or "hostages." If kids can't sit still because the seat of education is getting very antsy, that's not the time to drag out a big ol' heavy *King James* and announce you are going to read through the book of Lamentations. Often we used Walk Thru the Bible Ministries books written for families or The One Year Book of Devotions for Kids series.

## Bedtime Rituals

I cannot think of any time better spent than cultivating an evening ritual of baths and brushing teeth followed by Mom or Dad sitting on the edge of the bed, laughing, snuggling, talking, reading from the Bible or a Bible storybook, and fielding questions like, "Where did God come from?" Bedtime rituals with small children pay dividends well into the teen years.

When our children were toddlers, we wore out every children's Bible Kenneth Taylor had a hand in creating while we tucked those kids into bed. The first favorite was *The Bible in Pictures for Little Eyes,* featuring wonderful illustrations and a brief text, followed by three or four questions. The next favorite, and you know how favorites can change from week to week, was Taylor's *Big Thoughts for Little People.* Each page featured a letter of the alphabet. "A is for Adore." "K is for Kindness." "W is for Worship." Each page was richly illustrated and included text that explained the big idea and several questions that required careful observation of the marvelously detailed illustrations. All of those books still sit on our shelves today.

We also used the bedtime rituals to teach our children the mechanics of prayer. We told them that prayer is simply talking to God. Pray simple prayers with your children, encourage them to pray, and teach them to pray. And don't rush. The dishes will wait, voice mail can catch the phone, and odds are there's absolutely nothing on television worth watching. Don't rush. Of course, that's much easier said than done.

I remember the prayer of the small child who listed everything she was thankful for when she prayed before bedtime. She gave thanks for her Big Wheel and her teacher and the sheep on her wallpaper border and her pillow and her family and her family's family and for food and for the birds.

…and I was thinking, *Let's wrap this up soon; I have some things to do.*

And she was thankful for the rabbits and that she found the missing piece to Candy Land and for her toothbrush and for Linda, who sings praise songs in the car when she drives kids places.

…and I was thinking, *If she keeps this up, we're going to have to put a rug in here; this hardwood floor is killing my knees.*

And she was thankful for the rain and the sun and that the police officer with the radar gun didn't catch Mommy speeding and for Jesus and God and the Holy Spirit and, oh yes! she loves them the same and doesn't have favorites.

…and I was wishing this would come to an end soon when I was struck with the realization that I was wishing an end to a prayer of thanksgiving and praise to the God of the universe. Here was a child building a faith that would carry her through who knows what in the future, and I was willing to cut it short in order to get to my very important list of things to do.

I determined that I would never rush a kid again. Still, at times I'd get antsy during these rituals. Did they never tire of the same songs, the same prayers over and over? Not after a hundred times or a thousand times? No, never. And yet those five, ten, or fifteen minutes strengthened our relationship and planted the seeds of their relationships with God. Those few minutes often had a way of putting an entire day into perspective. We spend so much time living and planning for the next half hour, the next week, and the next holiday that the time we have today can slip away right under our noses.

## The Rhythm of Sunday

The third natural teaching time is Sunday morning. Corporate worship is part of our identity as a family. Getting up as a family, scrambling for a turn in the bathroom, leaving home as a family, and warming seats in the sanctuary together nurture our immediate relationships as well as our broader relationships within a community of faith. On Sundays children see a dimension to faith that they don't see at home. They see that Mom and Dad aren't the only ones who think faith is important. They see teenagers, twenty-somethings, middle-aged people, grandparents, and retirees who think faith is an important aspect of life.

Our family often sits in the fifth row from the back of the church. We used to sit right up front when our children were little. We thought if they knew they would be hauled out before the entire congregation, perhaps they would think long and hard before squirming, talking out loud, or making a scene.

Oh well, the main thing is that we all learn from our mistakes.

Since our children are now more young adults than children, and since they have pretty well mastered the art of sitting, we have yielded the more threatening seats to younger families in need of a little leverage.

Personally, I think you get a lot more out of church by sitting farther back.

For weeks we've been watching the progress of a family and their four little ones who totter in like so many tiny ducklings. The oldest is their biological son; the younger three were adopted from Romania. The smallest has dark brown hair and even darker eyes. During her first week in services, she clung to her mother's neck with a look of terror. She was afraid—of the people, the singing, the clapping, and especially the tambourine. Now she sits on a chair by herself. Her little head and shoulders sway in big wide circles as she claps in time with the music. If you ever doubted the power of love…

And none of us will ever forget the slight commotion near the center aisle during a rousing chorus of "Christ the Lord Is Risen Today" one Easter Sunday. It was Bill. Bill is a doctor, a specialist who sees a lot of the middle-aged men at our church.

He had his granddaughter with him. Four years old. Blue and white gingham-checked dress with a huge bow, white tights, and patent leather shoes. She was pulling at Bill's hand, tugging and pleading, "Dance with me, Grandpa, dance with me." Bill chuckled and demurely declined. No doubt Bill filled her dance card as soon as they returned home. Everyone should have the pleasure of knowing a dancing urologist.

Two rows directly ahead, a little boy climbed onto his momma's lap during prayer time. The two forms silently and gracefully molded into one. Not a single shaft of sunlight passed between the two. That momma had surgery for a brain tumor not too long ago. Now she's undergoing radiation. If you ever doubted the power of prayer…

One Sunday a couple recently transplanted from Africa to the Midwest shared a bit of their background. The husband is working on his doctorate in church history. He said it was the teacher in him that compelled him to project an overhead map of the world and offer a lesson in geography. He graciously pointed out that the United States is only one part of the world. He then asked why we call it the World Series when both teams come from the same country.

Many facets of community are seated in front of us—a struggling marriage, a heart condition, a woman recently widowed, and a family wrestling with unemployment and financial hardship.

Standing for the closing prayer, I caught a glimpse of a teenage girl as she slipped her arm around her mother's waist. It was one of those tender moments that dissolve into time all too quickly.

Not to slight the role of the pastor, but if you've been missing church as a family, you've been missing a lot more than a sermon. You're missing out on community.

Sunday-school lessons help cultivate the seeds of faith. They partner with, and reinforce, the teaching that happens at home. Material is approached in a methodical, thematic, or sequential manner without the distraction of ringing phones and the nagging question, Is there anything good to eat? Messy, gooey craft projects often accompany Sunday-school lessons, along with musical activities that many an artistically challenged or tone-deaf parent isn't able to pull off at home.

Sunday-morning services also build into the foundation of faith in that they create a rhythm to life. We work at our assorted jobs, tasks, and duties Monday through Friday, dash around like mad on Saturdays, running errands and playing catch-up, then pause on Sunday. We slow the pace, turn to God, offer thanks, and seek refreshment and strength for the week to come. Do you hear it? There's a rhythm to the week. Sustained activity punctuated by a day of rest. Sundays are part of God's plan to protect us from burnout.

As parents we hope that our children will feel that rhythm

long after they've left home. I've often thought that if our kids choose to sleep in on Sunday mornings after they've gone off to college, I sure hope they will feel something is missing. I hope they feel that the rhythm of their week is off kilter. I know, I know. It's not a particularly nice thought, but when a mother can't be there, she sends the next best thing: guilt.

Even in the routine of attending church, you never know what children catch, what passes overhead, or what goes directly in one ear and out the other. Was my teenage son really singing or just moving his lips? Is the kid fervently praying or sound asleep? The youngest *looks* as if she's listening, but is she *really* listening? You don't cultivate habits of faith because they come with a guaranteed success rate (they don't); you cultivate habits of faith because it's the right thing to do. You hope that a habit takes a strong hold and makes an impact on an attitude. In his autobiography, Ben Franklin referred to these as "habitudes."

We first had an inkling that the Sunday habitude might be beginning to sink in when the children were eight, six, and four. One particular weekend my husband was out of town, and I had a miserable head cold and a touch of the flu. I told the children that we wouldn't be going to church. They disappeared for a few minutes, then resurfaced and suggested we have church at home. All I had to do was throw on a pair of sweats and come when called.

A few minutes later I was summoned to the girls' upstairs

bedroom. They had moved their little wooden play table to the center of the room and covered it with a navy blue bath towel. An open Bible rested on top. The four little chairs that accompany the table had been lined up in a neat row. I was quietly seated and the service began when the six-year-old appeared in a wild getup from the dress-up trunk that would surely land her on Mr. Blackwell's Worst Dressed List. She was wearing a pink fur stole; a big, floppy straw hat; a long lavender skirt; red wooden beads; and pink and blue Barbie high heels made of 100 percent genuine plastic. She opened a Dr. Seuss book, which was a stand-in for a hymnal, and began to warble, creating lyrics off the top of her head as she crooned. When she finished she sat down in one of the chairs, leaned over, and asked if she had sounded like Mrs. Biggs. Mrs. Biggs is a family friend and soloist at our church who has a lovely soprano voice. I said, "Why, yes, of course you sounded like Mrs. Biggs." (I later apologized to Mrs. Biggs.)

Next, my eight-year-old son read a passage of Scripture. It was something out of the Old Testament that he had chosen at random. I don't remember what it was; I just remember being fascinated that they would attempt "church" on their own. The four-year-old sat on her little chair swinging her pudgy legs. We then sang a few praise choruses together and were dismissed with a benediction in the form of "Well, that's it!" It was one of the briefest and most memorable Sunday services I have ever attended. They had grasped the concept of setting aside time to honor God and the principle of worship. Bingo. Sometimes it works.

## Learn from My Mistakes

Looking back with 20/20 hindsight, I realize there are times I should have talked less and listened more—"Be quick to hear, slow to speak and slow to anger" (James 1:19). As parents, flawed and fallen human beings, we all make mistakes.

I have also had a tendency to shortchange the Holy Spirit. It doesn't matter what a phenomenal teacher you are, what a dynamic communicator you are, how loving a parent you are, or how strong your own faith is, you can't truly shape the inside of another human being's heart. Only the Holy Spirit can do that.

Another mistake I've made is to believe I'm more powerful than I am. I'm not saying I ever believed I was omnipotent, I'm just saying I can be a woman intoxicated by control. (Hey, I don't think I'm alone here.) I know now that a parent can teach, but no parent can force a child to learn. For a parent to assume total responsibility for the actions and character of a young adult is at best arrogant and pompous and at worst marginalizes the power of God.

A gifted orchestra teacher we have had the pleasure of knowing eloquently articulated yet another mistake of many well-intentioned parents. He says that Christian adults are like large, heavy-duty dump trucks, filled with huge payloads of belief, doctrine, creeds, convictions, knowledge, and information. They back up to kids and start dumping the entire load—totally forgetting that children are Yugos. Children are not ready to handle a load that big all at once. They don't have the power, the capacity, or the tread on their tires.

As a friend of mine remembers her mother frequently saying, "You can't put an old head on young shoulders." One of the best things we can do while steering Yugos and wrapping our arms around young shoulders is to help them gain experience. The best way for knowledge to travel that ten-inch road from the head to the heart is by way of experience. It's that slow, steady mix of knowledge and experience—the application of biblical principles into real life—that translates into mature faith. One of the most helpful things we can do as parents is to demonstrate with our lives how the principles of faith work. Don't just tell children about faith; show faith in action and bring them along. Pull them into the loop, be it raking the yard of a neighbor with cancer, taking a meal to someone who has been ill, cleaning house for a new mother, giving someone an afternoon out by baby-sitting her children, or dropping by a nursing home. It's always easier to learn by watching than by hearing.

If you live in a middle-class or upper-middle-class suburb,

one of the most beneficial experiences can be getting away from your own 'hood. Find ways to expose children to other cultures, other people, other times in history. Blaise Pascal, a renowned mathematician who was also a dynamic Christian and philosopher, said there are three ways to be well educated: one is through books, another is by understanding history, and the third is through travel. Sometimes you don't have to travel far; visiting a museum, a library, or an historic site, or simply seeing a different part of town can be highly educational.

The power of rituals and traditions stretches far into the future. Knowledge of God's Word plus real-time experiences that allow the knowledge to gel will more likely lead to a genuine faith than knowledge alone. The customs and routines that give rhythm to life create page after page in a child's bulging mental scrapbook. Maybe the rituals you create in your home will be so packed with power and fun that your children will carry them into adulthood, one day repeating the traditions in their own homes. A kitchen door swings open, grandkids you've yet to meet dive for cover, and a young father yells, "Honey, I'm home!"

# Chapter 5

# The Ugliest
# Plates You Ever Saw

*Doing All Things as unto the Lord*

· · · · · · · · · · · · · · · · · · · · · · · · ·

We have some plates in a kitchen cupboard that sits only inches above the floor. The plates are dark red, dull, scratched, and hard plastic. If you were to see the plates, you would quite naturally think, *Lori, where did you ever get such dog-ugly plates?*

Target. Fourteen years ago.

We have a nice set of off-white stoneware with blue trim and sprightly tulips in the center. Even so, for years the red plastic plates were our everyday workhorses. You can't hurt them. They're indestructible. I take that back. One did crack about four years ago. It wasn't the plate's fault. Someone had been using it for second base in a backyard ball game.

I bought the red plastic plates when our children were six,

four, and two. We'd finished dinner one night; I was exhausted and asked the older two to help clear the table. (I've always said my kids will help clear the table or my name's not June Cleaver.)

Since they were old enough to help set the table, I figured they were old enough to help clear it. But I soon realized I didn't want them doing it with my good stoneware, which is why I bought the cheap plastic plates the next day and put them in a cupboard beneath the counter where small children could easily reach them.

Part of our job as parents is doing things for our children, but a more critical part is teaching our children to do things for themselves. In essence, we nudge our children toward maturity. Parenting is a strange job in one regard. You're given these dependent, helpless, needy little creatures for whom you are completely responsible, and then it becomes your task to shape them into mature, independent young adults who can function on their own completely apart from you. Your success as a parent hinges on working yourself out of a job! We purposefully usher our kids through the different phases of childhood until they no longer need us. (And we wonder why we struggle with empty-nest syndrome?)

The English language is somewhat limited when it comes to the words we have to describe the different phases of childhood. The Hebrew language, however, contains a number of different words to describe these phases. Alfred Edersheim, in

*Sketches of Jewish Social Life in the Days of Christ,* identifies no fewer than nine different Hebrew terms, each depicting a fresh stage in the life of a child. The most descriptive word may be *naar,* which means "youth," or, literally, "he who shakes off or shakes himself free." Our job as parents is to point children in the direction of *naar.*

Parents help children shake free by teaching them a work ethic. When the apostle Paul penned a short letter to the church at Colossae, he included some practical advice on how families—and church members—can get along. During his discourse Paul urged his readers to work hard: "Whatever you do, do your work heartily, as for the Lord rather than for men" (Colossians 3:23). We pass on an important lesson when we teach our kids that all work is honoring to God when it's done heartily.

What kind of work? Any kind of work. Absolutely. Any kind of work (as long as it's not illegal or immoral) can honor God. A ten-year-old vacuuming out a car can be as honoring to the Lord as a nurse suctioning out the trach tube of a hospital patient. The homemaker scrubbing out a bathroom sink can tackle the task with the same enthusiasm as an investment banker giving financial advice. The homemaker may have to wear gloves and use a chisel to chip at the dried toothpaste, but still, work done well is honorable work.

Our views about work are most naturally learned within the confines of a family. We have a responsibility as parents to teach our children how to work and take on responsibility. We hamper our children's maturity when we do things for them that they can do for themselves. As a matter of fact, if we continually do for kids what they are able to do for themselves, chances are we'll raise a bunch of ninnies who may *never* consider leaving the nest. How's that for a scare?

## To Bribe or Not to Bribe

It takes backbone to teach a work ethic when you live in the Land of Ease. It's not as if we have to milk cows every morning at five, shuck corn, and beat the clothes clean on the rocks down by the river. Some weeks the most demanding manual labor I perform is to lug three gallons of milk into the house from the car. Not exactly what you'd call taxing.

I came across an article in the *Farmer's Almanac* that suggested that the next time you want your kids to clean, you should try hiding dimes throughout their rooms. Then make them "detectives" and tell them that if they clean their rooms right they'll find hidden surprises.

I wondered what type of parent would bait kids to clean their rooms. Actually, I knew what type of parent would try a suggestion like that—someone green, gullible, and extremely naive. Someone like me, who some years ago honestly believed that if I glued felt triangles and circles on a car-polish mitt, transforming it into a happy face, my then-four-year-old son would be interested in dusting. I sincerely thought that a fuzzy mitt with bright blue eyes, candy apple cheeks, and ruby red lips would make my little boy skip to the cleaning supplies, grab the mitt, and cheerfully dust every piece of furniture within reach, while warbling like Julie Andrews's little charges in *The Sound of Music*.

What can I say? He was my first child.

Shocker. Mr. Happy Mitt did not interest the four-year-old in dusting. Not a speck.

Mr. Happy Mitt was a dud. He was just the rude awakening I needed. I'd fallen victim to the thinking malaise that is peculiar to today's parents. For some strange reason, we feel compelled to make every facet of a child's life fun and entertaining by offering rewards, trinkets, candy, cash, and other incentives (please don't call them bribes—that sounds so crass) for accomplishing the routine and mundane.

We start by offering stickers to tots for landing their backsides on the potty chair. Then they grow accustomed to a toy with every hamburger. By second grade they expect a certificate and blue ribbon for participating in a round of Duck, Duck, Goose. I wouldn't be surprised if some teens lapse into shock when Twinkies are no longer passed out every time they complete a homework assignment.

Giving children an occasional positive reinforcement when

it has been well earned is smart parenting. But an indiscriminate barrage of trinkets, toys, and bribes quickly erodes into the price tag for compliance.

Pay a kid to do routine household chores? I've told my kids I'll pay them for doing chores the day I finish pressing their father's shirts and find a twenty-dollar bill at the bottom of the ironing basket.


## Assign Chores—They'll Thank You (Someday)

First Thessalonians 4:11-12 says, "Make it your ambition to lead a quiet life, to mind your own business and to work with your hands, just as we told you, so that your daily life may win the respect of outsiders and so that you will not be dependent on anybody" (NIV). People who work in a way that wins the respect of outsiders are increasingly rare today. Since thoughts about work are formed in the home, this sloppy attitude toward work reflects our culture's crumbling family structure.

Work is a huge component of every person's life, yet we often neglect to teach how work fits into a Christian worldview. When taught from a biblical perspective, work, like every other aspect of life—education, recreation, worship, family, prayer, relationships, Bible study, serving community, creating—lines up directly under God's reign.

We live in a post-Christian world. That means we live in a

world where the Judeo-Christian ethic, once a common de-nominator, has lost its punch. We live in a post-Christian world partly because we've lost sight of the fact that all things fall under the watchful eye of God. We've made a split between the sacred and the secular, artificially designating some activities as spiritual and some as nonspiritual. We have our secular world, which largely involves jobs, work, and careers that occupy the majority of the week and our waking hours, and then we have our spiritual lives—Sunday morning and maybe a midweek get-together now and then. We race through our secular tasks and jobs with our eyes on the spiritual things, thinking those are the things that matter most. There is no "matters most" in God's economy; it all matters. Likewise, the kingdom of God contains no secular and spiritual split. Christians live and breathe with the quiet intent of pleasing their Maker, whether they are hiking in the woods on a gorgeous autumn day, gro-cery shopping, double-checking figures on a spreadsheet, or struggling to stay awake during the seventeenth boring business meeting of the week. Our single greatest challenge as Christian parents is to heal that secular-versus-sacred split, to let our chil-dren see that everything we do is done before God. When we work heartily as unto the Lord, we restore dignity to work as well as to the worker. We intertwine the natural and supernat-ural, leaving no possibility of separation.

A child learns the value of work and responsibility by doing routine household chores, and doing them with an attitude of cheerfulness. (The cheerfulness is sometimes more an ideal than a reality, but where would we be without ideals?) Let the child know this is part of a Christian's witness to a watching world. By performing routine chores at home, we also show that we are part of the body of Christ.

> For the body is not one member, but many. If the foot says, "Because I am not a hand, I am not a part of the body," it is not for this reason any the less a part of the body. And if the ear says, "Because I am not an eye, I am not a part of the body," it is not for this reason any the less a part of the body. If the whole body were an eye, where would the hearing be? If the whole were hearing, where would the sense of smell be? But now God has placed the members, each one of them, in the body, just as He desired. (1 Corinthians 12:14-18)

In God's economy, every hand, foot, eye, ear, belly button, and little toe are important. It doesn't matter how insignificant a body part—or a job—may appear. What matters is working in a hearty and robust manner, which subsequently brings honor to God. Any job done heartily carries the distinction of dignity. When we ask kids to take out the trash, vacuum, dust, set the table, give their best effort in school, and trudge off to work with a good attitude, we cultivate within them a good work ethic.

When we let children bear responsibility for specific chores (that's code for work), we allow them to understand they are critical members of the team, first-string starters instead of benchwarmers. Over the years I've given the we're-a-team-and-you're-gonna-be-a-player speech with predictable regularity.

Two generations ago, when much of the population was still agrarian-based, a child began doing chores when he or she was big enough to carry a water bucket. Children knew they were key to the survival of their family. Today, with our streamlined, computerized, dot-com, e-lifestyles, children often end up being little more than spectators when it comes to the integral workings of a family. Most children aren't necessary to keep the wheels of a family turning, and they know it. They see it. They feel it.

As an adult I can take feeling unappreciated ten times easier than I can take feeling unneeded. Likewise, kids need to know that they are needed, that they are necessary, and that adults think they are capable of taking on work and responsibility. They may not articulate it, but children need the satisfaction of knowing they are contributing members of the household and the family.

When I was a little girl and spent time on my grandparents' farm, one of my jobs was to carry a big glass jar of milk from the milk house by the dairy barn back to the house. I knew that my grandma would be waiting for that jar. I could see the cream rising to the top as I sloshed my way down the long walk back toward the house. I walked briskly, passing the garage, the toolshed, the old outhouse, and the chicken coop. When I reached the house, Grandma would skim off the cream, saving it for my grandpa's coffee when chores were through, and put the milk into the refrigerator. The milk would rapidly disappear throughout the morning as it was poured into bowls of cereal or mixed into pancake batter. Carrying that jar made me a link in the morning chain of events. I was a part of helping the day get off to a good start. Satisfaction came with carrying that jar from the milk house. That simple act let me know I was a trusted worker and responsible helper.

Assign children jobs that are age appropriate. Little ones can help set the table, count out the napkins, hold the dustpan, and gather ingredients from around the kitchen. Older ones can help clean, spray Windex on mirrors, take out the trash, fold clothes, or unload the dishwasher. A stay-at-home mom can feel a need to justify her existence by doing all the housework. A smart stay-at-home mom will delegate not only in the interest of good time management but in the interest of nudging her children in the direction of maturity. Remember, Mom, it's not exclusively your home, and it's not *your* work. The home belongs to everyone in the family, and it takes everyone to keep the home and family running smoothly.

Praise children when they do their assigned tasks well. You don't have to stand on a chair and applaud, but do give a compliment and a thank you when they're earned. And, oh yes, keep your expectations realistic. "Thanks for getting a clean sleeper from the laundry basket so Mommy can change the baby. Maybe tomorrow I can teach you how to do the laundry. Hey! Come back here!"

"Thanks for setting the table. That helped keep the family on schedule tonight. It will be even nicer tomorrow night when you do it without slamming the cupboard doors."

"Thanks for cleaning out the car. It will make our trip to Ohio a lot more pleasant if we're not knee-deep in cracker crumbs."

Everybody wants to be valued. People feel valued when they know they perform an essential task. Let children know they're a needed and integral part of the family by having them help with simple everyday chores. They'll thank you for it. Okay, maybe not tomorrow, but eventually. Someday. In theory.

Developing a work ethic also cultivates the habit of honoring commitments—that old finish-what-you-start business. Today the commitment may be as simple as cutting the grass or finishing a book report on time. But another day, the commitment may be much larger in scope, a decision to honor a vow made "for better or worse, for richer or poorer, in sickness and in health, until death do us part." Do all things heartily as unto the Lord. It's an important component of faith. Just as God brings honor and dignity to the everyday man, so God brings honor and dignity to everyday work.

The story of Zacharias and Elizabeth, parents of John the Baptist, offers us an excellent example of God working in the midst of the everyday. Luke 1:8 says, "Now it happened that while he was performing his priestly service before God in the appointed order of his division…an angel of the Lord appeared to him."

What was Zacharias doing when an angel of God appeared and announced that he and his wife would bear a son named John? He was working. Just like you and me, Zacharias was going about his routine. He was working at his ordinary job, which happened to be serving as a priest. He was probably chipping away at a lengthy to-do list, following policies and procedures, when out of the blue—POW!—God sent an angel, and history was changed forever. It all happened in the breadth of that little word *while: while* Zacharias was working.

God still works through the ordinary, and He expects us to work through the ordinary as well. Children must learn that even simple work is significant. Some people live their lives yearning to do extraordinary things for God when God is right there beside them, waiting to work through the ordinary.

# Chapter 6

# "Napkin, Anyone?"

*Never a Day Without Forgiveness*

● ● ● ● ● ● ● ● ● ● ● ● ● ● ● ● ● ● ● ● ● ● ●

At our table no meal is complete without napkins. Napkins are terribly convenient for that dribble of taco sauce or the sudden explosion of laughter that sends a mouthful of corn on the cob flying across the table. A napkin, be it paper or cloth, performs clean-up duty and is indispensable for restoring some semblance of respectability to mealtimes.

In the spiritual realm, the napkin represents forgiveness. Forgiveness does clean-up duty in the relationships of life.

I'm a grown woman. I know the rules. I know what works and what doesn't. I know what's nice and not nice, appropriate and inappropriate, and yet I still blow it. I get ticked. I spout off. I jump to conclusions. I harbor a grudge. I freeze up like the Ice Queen. A sharp word, a bout of indifference, or an explosion reminiscent of Mount St. Helens. Hard to believe, isn't it? A nice gal like me.

Most of the time it's subtle, nothing any of the family could actually prove in a court of law—just your basic sulking, closing the oven door a little harder than necessary, and nursing a case of resentment deeper than the Pacific Ocean. I need forgiveness as much as I need six napkins with barbecue ribs. This snit-and-sulking thing I have been known to do turns out to be an inherited condition. The disease runs in both sides of the family. It's not tough to diagnose. Symptoms include selfishness, self-centeredness, complaining, grumbling, and manipulating to get your own way. The technical term for the disorder is *sin*. Our children, being from the same gene pool, have inherited the sin condition. The curly hair they inherited from me, the eye for detail from their father's side, but we both had a hand in passing on the tendency toward sin. Which is precisely why I sure hope we also pass on a few principles about forgiveness.

Sin and forgiveness go together like peanut butter and jelly. Naturally, the best way to teach children about the forgiveness of sin is to model it. Kids need to see adults extend forgiveness and receive forgiveness. They need to hear grownups around them say, "I'm sorry" and "I forgive."

## Living, Breathing, Blooming Examples

Two things happen when a parent apologizes and asks for forgiveness. First, by modeling forgiveness, we teach our children not only the importance of forgiving but the mechanics of forgiving. Second, we demonstrate obedience to God, because forgiveness lies at the crux of the Christian faith.

When was the last time your children heard you say you were sorry? Did their eyes pop out of their heads and their mouths drop open? Did they faint dead away on the hardwood floor? Did they yell, "Stay right there. I want to find my boom box and get this on tape!"

One spring I'd walked around to the side of the house to check on the peony bushes. Mom had given me starters from some of her own peony bushes in Missouri, some of which had come from her garden in Nebraska. Peonies are a hardy flower, sometimes living for nearly a century. This stock had crisscrossed the Midwest wrapped in newspaper and tossed in a cardboard box, and it was now about to thrive in the state of Indiana. I rounded the corner, anxious to see if the small balls that would eventually burst into gorgeous blooms were taking shape. There were no small balls on the peony bushes. There were hardly any peony bushes. My seven-year-old son, whom I had earlier been showing how to prune, had "pruned" the peony bushes. To the ground.

I tried to explain to him why you don't prune peony bushes *before* they bloom, and I wound up going ballistic. I was so mad about those bushes! Actually, I was mad about a lot of other things that day, and I unloaded it all on my son. I was lecturing and scolding about how I'd looked forward to those blooms, and now he'd hacked them off at the base, and what was he, *crazy?* It didn't take long to realize that I hadn't corrected him, I'd annihilated him. I'd torn into him as if he were a malicious master gardener sabotaging my garden instead of a little boy who didn't know the difference between an azalea and a hosta.

We were going somewhere in the car later that day. I'd calmed down and knew I needed to apologize, that I needed to apologize in front of the family because I'd gone nuts on him in front of the family. We were driving along when I turned around from the front passenger seat and said to my son in the far back, "I need to say something to you." He was looking out the back window. "What are you looking at that's more important than looking at me when I'm trying to talk to you?" I asked.

"A dead raccoon," he answered, tears running down his cheeks.

It was a moment of humbling that I truly deserved. If I'd been on the receiving end of an outburst like the one I'd delivered to him, I'd have found road kill a lot more pleasant to look at too.

In theory, the concept of forgiving or asking forgiveness sounds simple. But in some ways it's one of the most delicate forms of all human communications. Asking forgiveness requires the right attitude, the right approach, the right tone of voice, and the right timing. (I later apologized to my son when we could sit face to face. My apology was better timed and more sincere, and he readily forgave. *I love that boy!*)

Most adults find apologizing about as natural as paying income taxes with a smile. I can apologize to my kids without a lot of apprehension because I know they'll accept my apology. Maybe it's a gift of youth, but forgiveness seems to come easily for them. The hardest one for me to apologize to? My spouse. It's so much easier for me to go around thinking that my husband is the difficult one than it is to be honest and admit that I can be a jerk.

Too bad admitting I am wrong is so tough. A flood of power can be unleashed in those two simple words: I'm sorry. Apologizing can sweeten a sour relationship, cool a flash-point temper, or restore a broken soul's love for life. My husband and I have had to work at saying we're sorry and letting the kids hear us say we're sorry to each other. Knowing that we play by the same rule book when it comes to forgiveness has been key in getting past the arguments and friction that come with a marriage. It's also important to let children see how forgiveness works in the relationship between a husband and wife, because someday they'll face the same situation.

To better teach about the mechanics of forgiveness, we've laid out some ground rules for issuing the basic apology. The offender must make eye contact with the offended, identify the wrong, make restitution if possible—and apologize.

If someone borrows an article of clothing without asking (this can become a real hot point between sisters), the borrower must face the offended party, name the article of clothing that was heisted (*without* going into a lengthy explanation as to why it was the perfect top to go with the only pair of pants that were clean), apologize, return the article of clothing, and affirm that she will refrain from such behavior in the future.

Some days the plan works better than others.

Over the years we've heard the halfhearted apology that's uttered from a child's mouth as he or she vibrates the dry wall from the foundation while stomping away with the force of a sumo wrestler. "SAAAAAW-ry," the word is snarled with a hung head and curled lip. This is definitely not the real thing.

Other faux apologies we've heard include:

- The master manipulator who initiated an apology with a chipper "I'm sorry!" followed by a quick, but equally insincere "I love you!"

- The drama queen who could turn on the waterworks full blast and hurl herself into a chair, sobbing that she is worthless and inept. The chest would heave in and out, arms flailing, and hands dramatically sweeping hair out of the eyes. With an audience, the show would run about two minutes; without spectators, it was ten seconds tops. It was good stuff. For a while we were pretty sure this particular child would have a future in the dramatic arts.

Actually, our kids have pretty well gotten the hang of forgiveness. Sometimes I'll find a note on my bedside table, a letter on the computer desk, or a flower in a vase, all of which serve to say, "I'm sorry. Let's talk when things cool down." It's always touching when something like that happens because asking forgiveness has not been my strong suit. I may have helped plant the seeds in my children's hearts, but with the help of the Holy Spirit they grew the plants on their own.

## To Forgive or to Pout, That Is the Question

Adults are often worse than children at withholding forgiveness or an apology. Someone offends us, crosses us, breaks the rules, disappoints us—particularly our teenagers—and we want to squeeze just a little more out of it. Hash it over a few hundred more times, review the infraction in depth (preferably on stage under the spotlight, with me, myself, and I playing the mortally wounded). We have this need to remind everyone within earshot just how very, very, very much this really, really hurt.

Faced with the temptation of rehashing a past episode, I flash on the thought that this isn't how Christ forgave me. He never said, "I'm going to forgive you, but I'd just like to review this lengthy list of every deceitful and despicable transgression you've committed over the past five years and browbeat you a little more." No. Never. The psalmist says, "As far as the east is from the west, so far has He removed our transgressions from us" (103:12).

Adults like a clean slate, and children do too. It's like a cleansing rain after a week of blowing dust.

In addition to setting things right with one another, we also need to set things right on a vertical plane. When we sin or break God's commandments, we haven't just hurt another person, we've directly hurt God. David was keenly aware of this when he penned Psalm 51:4, "Against thee, thee only, have I sinned" (KJV).

I remember explaining this concept to my youngest, who was then about six. Not too many days later, I had a Momma Meltdown and overreacted about something. I apologized and asked if she would forgive me. She was gracious and said yes. A few minutes later I saw her sitting at the kitchen table, head bowed, eyes closed, hands folded. She was praying, "And dear God, You forgive her too."

We can't pass our faith on to our kids without passing on forgiveness, the cornerstone of Christianity. Without Christ's death on the cross, there would be no forgiveness, and without forgiveness, we would have no hope. No hope for eternal life, and no hope for this life.

Forgiveness offers hope for every important relationship adults or children form—relationships within the family, with friends, peers, college roommates, coworkers, neighbors, and business associates. Within forgiveness nestles the hope that our sins won't swallow us whole. We have the hope of restored fellowship with God, the hope of rebuilding broken relationships here on earth, and the supreme hope of life ever after.

## A Second Chance

Not only do we need to ask others for forgiveness, we also need to learn to accept forgiveness for ourselves. God offers it, but sometimes we hesitate to take it.

One of my favorite passages in the Old Testament is in the book of Jonah. God had commanded Jonah to go to Nineveh and preach repentance. But Jonah had no interest in going to Nineveh. In his mind God was asking him to cast pearls before swine. Jonah thought it would be better to hightail it in the opposite direction and hop aboard a ship. Which is exactly what he did. In response to Jonah's disobedience, God hurled a violent storm at the ship. When it started to break apart, the crew had to toss cargo overboard to lighten the load. Finally, after Jonah confessed that he was fleeing from the Lord's presence—and at Jonah's request—the crew heaved him overboard as well.

That led to the whale incident, which led to the three days and three nights amid the stomach acid, the spleen, and small intestines, which led to Jonah's crying out in desperation and being extremely sorry for what he had done. Whereupon the whale vomited Jonah onto the beach.

Jonah was sitting there examining his injuries, no doubt picking flecks of whale gut out of his hair, feeling miserable and plain awful about having tried to run from God, when along comes one of the best verses in the entire Bible: "Then the word of the LORD came to Jonah a second time" (3:1, NIV).

God gave Jonah a *second* chance! Jonah had had a change of heart. God knew it, and He came to Jonah offering him a fresh start. God will do the same for each one of us today. I want my kids to know that. I want them to know that when they've messed up little things or blown something big time, if they make a sincere U-turn back toward God, He will extend His hand a second time. Truthfully, I greatly enjoy being reminded of that myself.

Poet Robert Frost was also a fan of the story about the man in the belly of the fish. He said, "After Jonah, you could never trust God not to be merciful again."

"If we confess our sins, He is faithful and righteous to forgive us our sins and to cleanse us from all unrighteousness" (1 John 1:9). Never a meal without a napkin; never a day without mercy and forgiveness.

# Chapter 7

# Enchiladas
# Are Not Finger Food

*Cutting Everyday Problems into Bite-Size Pieces*

● ● ● ● ● ● ● ● ● ● ● ● ● ● ● ● ● ● ● ● ● ● ● ●

From time to time our children have argued about the necessity of silverware. One of them even tried to insist that enchiladas were finger food. No surprise. This was also the child known to take a slice of angel food cake, wad it into a ball, and eat it in one bite.

Forks and knives are what we use to cut our food into bite-size pieces. They are the utensils that prevent us from shoveling food in with both hands and hence making a spectacle of mealtime. In the spiritual realm we need a few knives and forks as well, some sharp utensils that will help us cut up large portions of worry, stress, and everyday trials into manageable pieces.

Jesus speaks at length about worry in Matthew 6:25-26:

> I say to you, do not be worried about your life, as
> to what you will eat or what you will drink; nor for
> your body, as to what you will put on. Is not life
> more than food, and the body more than clothing?
> Look at the birds of the air, that they do not sow, nor
> reap nor gather into barns, and yet your heavenly
> Father feeds them. Are you not worth much more
> than they?

And then He asks one of those marvelous rhetorical questions, which He promptly answers: "And who of you by being worried can add a single hour to his life?" (verse 27). Jesus gently chides listeners for worrying about things that are in the hands of God and for having meager faith. Then He admonishes, "Do not worry about tomorrow; for tomorrow will care for itself. Each day has enough trouble of its own" (verse 34).

When a day looks as if it has more than enough worry to fill the next twenty-four hours, it probably does. What a great time to pick up a knife and fork and cut life's super-size portions into bite-size pieces. And what a great time to teach a child how to manage adversity, be it a too-full schedule or a sudden disappointment from out of the blue.

## A Little Bit at a Time

All of us, children and adults alike, face trials and worries that must be faced head-on. It may be a broken friendship, a marriage that has hit a dry spell, or a betrayal you never thought possible. It may be financial hardship, a business deal gone bad, or the dreaded word *cancer*.

The concerns that confront children may sometimes seem insignificant or trivial to an adult, but they are nonetheless very sizable to a child. A book report or a papier-mâché relief map of Peru can be overwhelming. Pressure on the athletic field can generate considerable tension. The challenge may be strictly social, such as not fitting in at a lunch table, being shut out at recess, feeling pressure to have the perfect teenage body, or receiving no invitation to the big party.

These school, sport, and social obstacles can be a child's first tastes of adversity on a small scale. These situations provide opportunities for kids to gain practice and experience for facing off against the larger, and often far weightier, challenges of adulthood. Successfully tackling a mammoth science-fair project—especially when all the *other* kids have scientists and engineers for parents and all yours has are a couple of journalists—may one day prove invaluable when your child faces a challenge of far greater magnitude. When we give our children experience in undertaking something that seems far too big to handle—teaching them to break down a challenge into smaller components and work through them one at a time—we will equip them to face more daunting challenges in the not-so-distant future.

For example, my husband and I have often helped a certain someone who tends to melt down at exam time. She insists that the review sheets are Draconian, the book is unintelligible, and that the terminology must have been covered the day she went to the restroom for thirty seconds. But with a little prodding from us, she eventually sees how she can carve what looks like a giant mound of work into manageable pieces.

"You have three cell-division review sheets to study? Review the first one for fifteen minutes, and then have your sister quiz you. Then do the second review, and then the third. You'll be finished in under an hour."

With a parent's touch, sometimes even social problems can be broken into manageable parts. "Maybe you don't have anyone to sit with at lunch because you haven't made enough friends. This Saturday, why don't you have someone over? Maybe you can invite one new friend over every other week."

"I see those four grocery bags in your room are loaded with college brochures and catalogs. It looks overwhelming. Why don't you sort out your top ten this weekend? By the end of the school year, you can weed out a couple more, and this summer we can visit your top three."

Some children may share the obstacles in their path with you at the time they face them; others may not tell you until six years after the fact. One of our daughters was in middle school before she told us that she was so worried about doing well in first grade that she was scared to bend over to tie her shoe. "I was afraid I'd miss something the teacher said."

My heart was pierced. That worry was such a needless waste. She'd been fearful and distraught at school when she could have been calm and relaxed. Having a broader perspective on first grade, we could have assured her that she would survive all six years of elementary school even if she bent over every ten seconds to tie her shoe, but she never clued us in. Because she was an excellent student, we assumed everything was fine. I wish now that we'd asked a few more questions, taken more time to listen. Just because things look as if they're going fine doesn't necessarily mean your kids are fine on the inside.

## "Help Me Through This Day — Or the Next Half-Hour"

Of course, some children face adversities of a far different nature. Our son encountered a sizable challenge in sixth grade. For several years, when he was running or playing basketball or soccer, his left knee would suddenly buckle and he would collapse. He'd experience intense pain. We'd ice the knee for a while, and then he would resume normal activity. A doctor who examined the knee said our son was fine.

One President's Day, a school holiday, he was shooting hoops with a group of neighbor kids in the driveway. I'd heard the ball thump, thump, thumpin' against the backboard for close to an hour. I was working in the house and was vaguely aware that the thumpin' had stopped. A neighbor boy ran inside and said, "You'd better come. Jeremy's knee went out and he can't get up."

When his knee buckled, the kneecap completely dislocated. I could see by the ripple of my son's blue jeans that the kneecap was dangling to the side of his leg. It was a grotesque image that has yet to completely fade from memory.

We rushed him to the emergency room, and within an hour, a doctor had rolled the kneecap back into place. The doctor went over the procedure with us twice. "Have your son lie flat and extend his leg like this," he said. "Then you hold the heel in the palm of your hand and give the kneecap a tap. Most times it will snap back into place." I wondered why in the world he was telling us that. Surely we'd have no reason to use such information again.

An orthopedic surgeon gave the kid a once-over the next day in his office. He slapped the x-ray from the emergency room onto a lightbox, took a brief look, and said, "Wow!" I'm of the persuasion that it's never a good sign when a surgeon looks at an x-ray and says "Wow!" It's usually an indication you're going to be helping the man buy a boat or put one of his kids through graduate school. My inkling was right. The doctor said our son had flat kneecaps that were prone to dislocate and that he would need surgery.

The leg was in a neon-colored cast for four weeks as we waited for muscle tears to heal and the swelling to go down so the surgeon could operate. Surgery was followed by another cast (bright blue) for four weeks, which was followed by a splint with steel rods for two weeks. Physical therapy started the day our son came home from surgery.

He had to do two different sets of leg lifts three times a day and ice the knee between rounds of lifts. Thirteen-year-old males can be among the world's most difficult convalescents to work with. In the kid's defense, he was facing a tough challenge. We couldn't do the exercises for him, nor could we bear the pain for him. All we could do was encourage him. "Just take it a step at a time. No pun intended. Don't worry about playing soccer; don't worry about next month or next week. Just focus on what you have to get through today." We told ourselves the same things we were telling him.

Once the cast was removed, he began physical therapy five days a week. In addition to therapy at the clinic, he did exercises at home. When progress was slow in coming, the physical therapist gave us a small black box to take home. Inside the box were a couple of dials and wires with electrodes to hook up to our son's thigh muscles. You flip a switch, and a jolt of electrical current stimulates the muscle. Our days were consumed with driving to and from physical therapy, exercising and icing at home, and now the Frankenstein routine.

One day after he had the electrode treatment, he was lying on the floor totally and completely discouraged. Struggling to find some form of encouragement, as this one-day-at-a-time business had now expanded to months, I got down beside him and said, "I bet you're wondering why God let this happen. I don't know why He let you have flat kneecaps. But I do know that He uses times like this to build character."

My son looked at me, his eyes welling with tears, and said, "But I don't want to learn character!" I thought, *Yeah, you and me both, Bud.* It was all I could do to keep from crying myself. Not many of us welcome the sizable challenges that can build character.

But sometimes it's only when we come face to face with our own complete and utter helplessness that we turn to God to ask for His strength. We realize we're not nearly as in control as we thought we were. Our limitations become crystal clear. Prayers quickly turn from "Help me through the week, Lord" to "Help me through this day, Lord" to "through the afternoon, through the next hour, and through the next five minutes."

When we come to the end of ourselves, we realize the only lasting reservoir of strength comes from God. Paul writes about praying three times for a physical affliction to be removed from him. He wasn't given any relief. Instead, he had to learn to cope with the pain. Paul cast the situation in terms of strength and weakness.

> And He has said to me, "My grace is sufficient for you, for power is perfected in weakness." Most gladly, therefore, I will rather boast about my weaknesses, that the power of Christ may dwell in me. Therefore I am well content with weaknesses, with insults, with distresses, with persecutions, with difficulties, for Christ's sake; for when I am weak, then I am strong. (2 Corinthians 12:9-10)

What an exchange program! God's strength for my weakness. His power for my fear.

Our son had experienced a full recovery just as the new school year was starting. He played indoor league soccer and resumed an appropriate level of rambunctiousness for a middle-school boy. The next spring he was tossing a football in the back-yard when he jumped up to catch a pass, came down, and collapsed. The same knee dislocated again. He was able to instruct his friend how to snap the kneecap back in place. He'd been listening to the doctor that night in the emergency room, listening to the information I was so certain we'd never need again.

This time, we knew what was ahead. I wish I could say that made it easier, that we skated through the process with smiles on our faces. But knowing what was ahead didn't make it any easier. In fact, knowing the length of recovery only made it more grim. We did the only thing we could—we took it one bite at a time.

All told, our son has endured four total dislocations (two on each knee—at least he's symmetrical). He's had casts in every color of the rainbow, countless splints, three surgeries, and untold hours of physical therapy. He now boasts matching five-inch scars on both legs.

With each trip to the surgeon's office, I could feel our son looking at our faces. I knew that if we flinched, he'd flinch. He was taking his cues from us. If his parents faced adversity with faith and kept the panic to a minimum, it would encourage him to do the same. He didn't just study our faces in the surgeon's office; he studied us on the way home. I've never felt so scrutinized, and I've never felt such an obligation to be strong on someone else's behalf.

With each dislocation, we did grow a little more somber. But there was no way out; we simply leaned into the wind and took it one day at a time. We couldn't roll three months of pain, sweat, and hard work into one day of worry. We couldn't take a shortcut, couldn't get from point A to point Z by skipping over B through Y. While what we'd already been through didn't make the third dislocation, surgery, and rehab any easier, it did something else: It gave us the confidence that we would get through it. Sometimes, when the pain and circumstances don't make sense, endurance itself is ample reward. Psalm 9:9-10 says,

> The LORD also will be a stronghold for the oppressed,
> A stronghold in times of trouble;
> And those who know Your name will put their trust in
>     You,
> For you, O LORD, have not forsaken those who seek You.

Our trust was in the Lord, that He would replace our impatience with His patience and that we would get through this by taking it one moment at a time. Dislocated kneecaps pale in light of more serious situations—situations where there is no surgical fix or three-month recovery.

## A Story of Trust

We have a family friend whose youngest child has a mysterious neurological disease that falls somewhere under the heading of muscular dystrophy. His connective muscle tissue is extremely weak. If you wipe off David's hand after a meal, it feels, and appears, as if it will completely separate from his wrist because it is so loosely connected. When you scoop him up in your arms, he becomes a little floppy as his arms and legs dangle freely. The best way to describe David is that he's like a marionette puppet with loose strings. He doesn't have the strength to support his body weight. Even when David sits in his wheelchair, he sometimes needs help moving his legs to get comfortable. The strength David does have is embedded in his smile. It's a 500-watt flash of brilliance that lights up a room. David has a great disposition and is one of the kindest, sweetest, most appreciative nine-year-olds I have ever had the joy of knowing. David is a little boy with big faith.

David's father and mother, Damian and Sally Neeld, are people of faith too. Despite a firm foundation, they readily admit that on some days the problems before them look insurmountable. Sally says the key for them is to look at daily life through eternal eyes: "We have to remember that we're just here on earth for such a short time, a mere vapor compared to all eternity. Each day we have to take care of the demands that are at hand for that particular day. God has taught us that we can't do this without His power in our lives. It's only through His strength and power, and allowing Jesus to live through us, that we're able to get through each day."

Sally is a petite woman with a slender build. Her daily

routine is inseparable from David's. While her husband, Damian, and their two other children, Robby and Katie, are a big help, some days Sally cares for David by herself for the most part. A lot of "David lifting" goes on in the course of Sally's day. She gets David up, helps with his bathing and dressing, gets his breakfast, rolls him to the garage in his wheelchair, and then lifts him into the van. She walks around to the back, folds his wheelchair, and hoists it into the van. She drives him to school, lifts him out of the van, and situates him back in his wheelchair. At midafternoon the process begins in reverse. Sally and Damian become David's arms and legs in a thousand different ways. David had a growth spurt this past summer. He's doing what all nine-year-old boys naturally do—he's getting bigger and heavier.

"David is a delight," Sally says. "God has used him to strengthen our faith and mature us. Both Damian and I, and our whole family, are in awe over the fact that God would bless and use us like this. I feel honored that God would choose us to raise a little boy who has so many physical needs. I think, *God, why do You think I'm so capable of this?* Evidently, He's able to look down and say, 'These people can do this.'

"And," she continues, "whenever I start to feel as if the day is becoming overwhelming or too much, immediately God will remind me, whisper in my ear, 'There are people who have it so much worse.' I shake my head and think, *Yeah, this is nothing compared to what some people are going through. This is nothing compared to being homeless, without a roof over your head, or in some country where people don't know where the next meal will come from or how they'll stay warm in the winter.* I look at my life and think, *Man, I've got it pretty good.* God is faithful to help me look at the bright side."

Sally battles to keep a good attitude and strong faith. Nighttime can be particularly hard. "I think when we start to fall asleep, our defenses let down, and we're not as strong. Arrows from the Enemy are somehow able to get though in that semisleep state. One thing that has helped is being able to say, 'These thoughts are not from God; these thoughts are from the Enemy.' If I pursue those thoughts, I'll slip into depression. If I let those thoughts take hold, I'll start to worry about the future—what if David gets heavier, how will we lift him? What if this happens, what if that happens? Yet I'm always amazed the next morning when I get up and everything is still the same. You just can't think about the future. You have to plan and be responsible, but you can't think of all the what-ifs, because those are tomorrow's problems."

The Neelds always get an encouraging boost when they remember Ephesians 3:20, "Now to Him who is able to do far more abundantly beyond all that we ask or think, according to the power that works within us."

"The part that gets me," Sally says, "is that God blesses beyond what we even *think* about."

## Children Are Watching

David is a boy with a disability, but he is also a boy with optimism, hope, and faith. Those qualities have been contagious; David caught them from his parents. Children watch how parents face difficulty, how we square off with life's challenges. Children look to see if we panic or if we stay calm and refuse to bite off more than we can chew. They watch to see if we come totally unglued or whether our faith provides a secure port in the raging storm. They look to see if we divide the burden, parceling out the unknown and the uncertain to God.

God desires that our faith be built on trust. Worry is the opposite of trust. Yet worry comes naturally to many of us, particularly to women. We used to tease my mother-in-law about transforming worrying into an art. She worried over potential dangers involving ropes, ladders, anything wired for electricity, people in the bathroom too long, and all manner of weather alerts.

She didn't believe the cliché that most of the things we worry about never actually happen. She believed worrying was what prevented bad things from happening. Proof in point: No one in her family had ever been struck by lightning, sucked down the toilet, or abducted from a parking lot because they insisted on buying milk after dark. She'd grin, wink, and claim that she worried us all into safety. She also had a prayer list tucked in her Bible that she covered faithfully.

Mothers can worry about the past: Did I discipline enough, too much, not enough? Were my children deprived because we didn't have cable television when they were little? Do they hate fish because of my cooking, or do they just hate fish?

Mothers can worry about the future: Will my parents enjoy good health in their golden years? Who will my children marry? Will they be able to hold a job? Will they one day write a book sensationalizing my life as the imperfect parent? Will they wear a seat belt and eat green vegetables when I'm not around to nag?

Most of all, mothers worry about the present: Is that a simple cough or double pneumonia? How long would he really go without cleaning his ears if left on his own?

Few among us would volunteer the number of hours our minds are occupied with worry. Instead, we shrewdly disguise our worrying with more acceptable labels like "concerns" and "observations."

But God sees the worry in our hearts. He also knows how we're tempted in the night to play out the worst possible scenarios. Aware that we often wear our hearts on our sleeves and by so doing have the ability to pass on our neurotic tendencies to our children, He gave the strong admonition of 2 Corinthians 10:5

(which should probably be titled "For Women Who Worry"): "We demolish arguments and every pretension that sets itself up against the knowledge of God, and we take captive every thought to make it obedient to Christ" (NIV).

If we round up those stray thoughts that frighten us and scare us, taking them captive and tossing out the ones that bear no likeness to Christ, our children may learn to do likewise.

When we refuse to take our fears captive to Christ and insist on shoving worry in with both hands, we must look like pigs at the trough. Learning to cut a heaping serving into manageable portions is the foundation of trust. It's the best way to get our hands around that concept of living one day at a time and leaving tomorrow's worries for tomorrow.

Teach your children how to handle challenges and adversity. Exercise trust, release the worry, and take each day one bite at a time.

# Chapter 8

# The Big Hug Mug

*A Swig of Humility*

● ● ● ● ● ● ● ● ● ● ● ● ● ● ● ● ● ● ● ● ● ● ● ●

I cradle in my hands a plump, honey-colored coffee mug. On at least four different occasions, I have taken this mug to the trash, pitched it, and then twenty seconds later gone back and fished it out. I have never particularly liked the mug, but I feel compelled to keep it for historical purposes. Let me explain.

Second grade was not a stellar year for our firstborn child. There was a ten-day period that was positively awful. Even though he was sweet, adorable, and the most perfect child in the entire universe, I was sure he was headed to juvenile hall. (By the way, I have permission to share these stories. The children have consented, and the statute of limitations expired long ago.) Remember, this boy was our first child, so for the first, oh, ten or twelve years, overreaction on my part was pretty much the norm.

The kid did three things back-to-back that I thought were shocking. (Silly me. I had no imagination as to what potential the teen years would offer.) The first incident occurred when my husband and I went to visit our son's second-grade class. My husband and I made it a practice to do this every year in elementary school. It gave us a mental picture of where our child was during the day. We could meet the teacher, check out the environment, and make sure there was order in the classroom.

My husband had taken the morning off work. We drove to the school, walked down the long hallway to the second-grade wing, and arrived at the classroom right behind the vice principal, who was walking at a brisk pace with her high heels clicking sharply on the tile floor. She clutched two green slips in her hand. We overheard her tell the teacher that she needed to talk to two boys—one of them being our son.

"Hello," we said. "Is there a problem?"

"Well, yes," she said. "Your son and a friend were wrestling on the floor of the bus this morning. The bus driver gave them both a citation."

For a parent, the only thing worse than humiliation before one of your peers is humiliation in front of twenty-five little kids staring at you with faces that say, "And who thought the two of *you* had the brains to become parents?"

The vice principal continued, "Normally I'd take the boys down to my office and scare the livin' daylights out of them, but since I know you, and I know you'll take care of the matter at home, we can just leave it at this."

"We will take care of it at home," my husband said. "But please, feel free to take him down to your office and scare the livin' daylights out of him anyway."

"We'd appreciate it," I said.

My husband and I had always known we didn't want to be the type of parents who believed their kids could never do any wrong. We wanted our children to learn by taking their lumps. What we *didn't* know was that, for parents, this could be rather embarrassing.

We both blushed and considered crawling out of the school on all fours. It would be the first of several trips out of the building that year that I made with my tail between my legs. By the end of the year, when a voice would ask, "Are you Jeremy's mom?" I had two automatic impulses. The first was to run. The second was to say, "Who's asking, and why do you want to know?"

In any case, the vice principal dealt with our son at school, and that evening we dealt with him at home. I was certain he was well on the path to reform, when two days later the phone rang. It was a new neighbor from one block over.

"Did your son wear a turtleneck to school today?" she asked.

"I think so," I said.

"Is it green?"

"Forest green," I said.

"I thought so," she answered. "I'm calling because I can see his head and shoulders bouncing above my neighbor's fence. Yep, there he goes again. My neighbor is out of town and—there he goes again—your son and a buddy went into her backyard without permission and are jumping on her trampoline. I'm watching them—there he goes again—right now from the window of my family room and thought you'd want to know. I know my neighbor doesn't want kids on the trampoline when she's not home."

I thanked her for calling, hung up the phone, and earnestly hoped she wouldn't tell the entire subdivision that my son was guilty of breaking, entering, and bouncing.

We had a little "discussion" when he got home—entrapment was probably more like it. I asked why he was late. He told a whopper, and I nailed him.

I was grateful to my neighbor for calling. We never told our children who the informant was. I suspect that we got a lot of mileage out of that over the years, with all of them knowing our neighbors might be spying on them from behind curtains or cracked doors.

## The Pain and Pleasure of Community

When we moved to Indiana with our small brood, my husband and I had hoped we would find a neighborhood with a sense of community. A place with sidewalks, streets lined with maple trees, and next-door neighbors who took in your paper when you went out of town. We wanted to live in a neighborhood where someone a block over would feel free to call if she saw your kid doing something out of line, and you'd feel free to call her in return.

Hanging up the phone, I realized we'd found just such a community. My neighbor had called to rat out our kid, and I was sincerely appreciative. Maybe one day I could return the favor. I kept an eye on her three kids for the next ten years. Unfortunately they never did a thing that warranted a call back.

Several days after the trampoline incident was Halloween. The kids were decked out in their costumes. Our jack-o'-lantern sat on the front porch doing its traditional spooky rolling-fog routine courtesy of dry ice and hot water. This year was my husband's turn to stay home and pass out candy to the three-foot monsters that came to the door, while I took the kids around the neighborhood. Naturally, this would be the same neighborhood where we welcomed accountability and community.

The kids rang the doorbell of a house on a cul-de-sac that backs up to our house. The man answered the door and said, "Oh, hello. I'd like to talk to you about your son the woodcutter."

"Pardon me?" I said.

His wife said, "Not now, John. Not now. This is not an appropriate time."

I said, "Now, John. Please, right now. If my son did something, I want to know about it." I was lying. I didn't really want to know about it. I'd had enough to last for the month, but as a mother, I was obligated to get on with the ugly side of life.

The neighbor continued, "Your son and his buddy think they're woodcutters. The other day they were outside and cut down three eight-foot white pine trees at the back of my yard. I liked those trees, and I like to watch the birds out there."

I apologized profusely, made sure the kids got their miniature Snickers bars (because I knew it was probably the last time they'd be getting candy from this house), and we made record time getting home.

In an animated fashion, I told my husband what had happened. We found a flashlight and headed out back. Our properties are separated by fences with a four-foot-wide easement between them. The kids used the easement to cut from one house to another and called it the Secret Passageway. Our kids weren't allowed to go past a cable box in the Secret Passageway. We began making our way through the Secret Passageway, trampling over brush and thickets in the pitch black, aided by a flickering beam from a flashlight with anemic D batteries. We walked and walked, waaaaay past the cable box, around a corner, down a lengthy straightaway and there they were—three spindly white pines, flat as you please.

I was a tad upset by the time we got back to the house. I was so nearly out of my mind that I made the silly mistake any mother with her wits about her knows not to make. I asked my son why.

"WHY?" I cried, wailing like a police siren.

He looked at me in my disheveled and frantic state and said, "George Washington cut down trees, and I don't remember him getting in a lot of trouble."

"Go to your room before I hurt you!" I said.

I then went to my room, sobbed uncontrollably, and called my mother long distance. I explained the latest addition to his rap sheet and asked her the same question, "Why? Why? Why?"

My mom paused and said, "Because he's a kid, Lori. Because he's a kid."

My heart melted like a Hershey bar in the glove compartment of the car in the middle of August. I was overwhelmed with my mother's response. I was overwhelmed because if you knew me growing up, you'd know what she *really* wanted to say was, "You're finally getting what you deserve!"

My mom was gracious and reassured me that while these events merited attention they were within the range of normal.

The next day, still feeling glum and envisioning my precious little boy in an orange jumpsuit behind a metal gate and iron bars, I saw an FTD truck pull into the driveway. There was a knock at the door, and the delivery man thrust a Pick-Me-Up bouquet into my hands. The bright carnations and daisies came in a large, honey-colored coffee cup that said "Big Hug Mug." It was from my parents. They'd already been down this road. They knew the disappointment and frustration, but they also knew it was nowhere close to the end of the world. So now you know why I have the love-hate relationship with the mug. We refer to it as the cup of humility. And over the years, like most parents, we've belted down more than a swig or two.

## A Teachable Spirit

To be a parent is to be made humble. There will be times when you are humbled by the things your children do. There will be times when your children will catapult you directly from humbled to humiliated. There will be times when you don't want to hear about the things your children do. Listen anyway! Listen to what's being said even if you think the other party (a) has a bad attitude, (b) is a crackpot, or (c) is simply jealous that your children all have perfect teeth.

Listen to the criticism, mull it over, consider whether there might be any truth to what is said, and then respond accordingly. It's called having a teachable spirit. It's imperative that you, as a parent, have a teachable spirit because if you don't, chances are good your child won't either.

In Scripture, the opposite of a teachable spirit is an unbowed head or a "stiff neck." A stiff neck represents insubordination and disobedience. Someone who refuses to listen to criticism or take correction is a "stiff-necked" person. God does not look kindly on the stiff-neck personality: "I have seen these people," the LORD said to Moses, "and they are a stiff-necked people. Now leave me alone so that my anger may burn against them and that I may destroy them. Then I will make you into a great nation" (Exodus 32:9-10, NIV).

Stephen's remarks to the Sanhedrin hit even closer to home: "You stiff-necked people, with uncircumcised hearts and ears! You are just like your fathers: You always resist the Holy Spirit!" (Acts 7:51, NIV).

A sign of maturity and humility is admitting that we all have blind spots. Some years ago I found it interesting to learn that while we talk about blind spots in attitudes we also have blind spots physically. Everyone has a blind spot in each eye. It's literally a blind spot because it is that small portion of the retina where there are no cells to transmit sight. The blind spot is the pinpoint area where nerves from the retina bundle together, form the optic nerve, and wind their way to the brain.

There's a simple exercise you can do to locate your blind

spot. Get a three-by-five-inch index card and put a small *x* and a dot about an inch and a half apart in the middle of the card. Holding the card in your right hand, cover your left eye with your left hand and slowly move the card toward your nose, focusing on the figure on the left. You will see both the *x* and the dot for a while, but as the card gets closer to your face, the figure on the right will briefly disappear. You've found your blind spot. How good of God to remind us literally of what we sometimes suffer from mentally. This isn't a bad little exercise to do with a child who suffers from an unteachable spirit and an unwillingness to be humble.

We can all suffer from blind spots, and most of us have a predisposition toward being stiff-necked. Being stiff-necked does not create a friendly atmosphere for humility and teachability. A teachable spirit will be most important during those times when your child refuses to listen to you. Hard to believe, but it's possible there will be a time when your child shuts you out. Cold and completely. That's when you pray—and if a child has a teachable spirit, God may very well be able to speak to a heart that has refused to listen to you.

A teachable spirit means being willing to own up to mistakes and face the consequences of our actions. Centuries ago Paul wrote to the Galatians, "Do not be deceived, God is not mocked; for whatever a man sows, this he will also reap" (6:7). Paul was writing about natural consequences, reaping the rewards or consequences of the actions we have sown. My husband and I wanted to be parents who would be humble enough to let children experience the zing of natural consequences. Our son's woodcutting expedition was a doozy of a sampler.

In the boy's defense, every spring he'd seen his dad clear brush out of the easement between our properties. These white pines were growing in such an easement, but that wasn't enough to justify what he'd done. He'd taken tools without asking. He'd gone way beyond his boundaries without asking. And he'd harvested timber without a logger's permit. We let the consequences fly.

## Truth and Consequences

The first painful consequence was that our firstborn had to look up a nursery in the phone book. The kid hated to alphabetize. He had to call a stranger and ask what white pines were selling for these days. The second painful consequence was going to the bank and drawing money out of his savings account. The third painful consequence came the next Saturday when he and his father (his mother was still too emotional to do this part) returned to the neighbor's home and rang the doorbell. Our son apologized and said that he would be working behind the neighbor's fence again, only this time planting instead of sawing. Our son's partner in crime experienced a similar scenario at his house and, hence, also participated in the reforestation effort.

Embarrassing? Yep.

Maddening? A bit.

Humiliating? Give it a 10.

Beneficial? Extremely.

We may have felt uncomfortable, but who cares? Good parenting isn't about feeling good as a parent; it's about doing the right thing. We tried to do the right thing, and as a result, the kid knew we meant business. He knew his actions would have consequences.

We improve our effectiveness as parents by refusing to run defense for our children. We need to take off the shoulder pads and chest guards and let our children feel the sting of the consequences of their actions. It may be embarrassing from time to time to you as the parent. Yes, you, the one who believed your little Do-No-Wrong would be class president, hall monitor, or the kid who wrote *other* kids' names on the board for talking when the teacher was out of the room, but never, *never* the kid who was called to the vice principal's office for misbehaving on the bus.

To learn from natural consequences is to be inducted into God's primary method of teaching. Over and over in the Old Testament, God called to the Israelites saying, "Obey Me, follow My commands, and be blessed—or disobey, ignore My commands, and experience the consequences of going your own way." The principles of sowing and reaping are as old as the cedars of Lebanon.

When your child gets caught red-handed at _____ (fill in the blank) or _____ (fill it in again), these are embarrassing times, but they are also beneficial times—if parents can step aside and not stand between the child and the consequences.

Letting children feel the sting of consequences when they are little is a lot easier than waiting until they are teens. By the time they reach adolescence, the nature of the activities and interests that may allure them (drinking, drug abuse, premarital sex) pose far greater, far more painful, and far more long-lasting consequences.

We've tried to practice natural consequences throughout our years as parents. So you're wondering, was second grade the last time this boy got into trouble? Let me put it this way: Do I look like a tall, blonde swimsuit model? I can save you the trouble of checking; the answer is no. Not too many of us, adults or children, have a learning curve that steep.

When children have a run-in with sin, it's productive for them to experience the consequences. It's a teachable moment that cultivates a teachable spirit. And that opportunity holds sweet promise even as we parents take another gulp from the cup of humility.

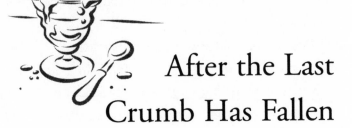

# Chapter 9

# After the Last Crumb Has Fallen

*Keep Things in Perspective and Persevere*

● ● ● ● ● ● ● ● ● ● ● ● ● ● ● ● ● ● ● ● ● ● ● ●

When everyone has left the table and all that's left are dirty plates, chairs askew, and the echoes of laughter, I like to pause and reflect on what just happened. Leaning on the counter and looking at the table, I see a multitude of shadows. There are images from the meal just passed: animated discussions, news tidbits, and the latest escapade with Spirit Foam in the high-school parking lot. A longer look reveals memories that linger from every stage of parenting: baby food jars, a cake with two candles, finger foods, knock-knock jokes, details about slumber parties, new braces, and contact lenses.

In those quiet moments, when the kitchen is empty or the house deserted, we can reflect and reach for some measure of objectivity concerning the flurry of activity around us. As I have attempted to put contemporary family life into perspective, some patterns have become exceptionally clear. Speaking from the vantage point of a mom who's been around the block a time or two, may I tell you what I see?

A lot of parents today are devoted and attentive to the infant, the toddler, and the elementary-school child. They're careful about monitoring health habits. "No preservatives or artificial coloring in my child's system!"

They screen the environment, filter junk from the media, preview movies, approve videos, pay attention to the music their little ones listen to, and are cautious about television. They're great at logging face time, talking together, hanging out together, and eating together. They seem to be on top of things.

But once middle school and high school hit, those things become harder. The task of sustaining a healthy and nurturing family life grows more difficult. Parents figure they've done all they need to do as parents. At this juncture a lot of parents simply cave. Thinking the battle to raise healthy, wholesome young adults is over, they give up and give in. Those who don't give up have a rough uphill climb ahead.

Sports and extracurricular activities fragment the family calendar. Kids start socializing more. They spend more time with their own generation and less time with other generations.

Adolescents are pulled in a hundred different directions, ninety-nine of which seem to lead away from the family. Movies, concerts, malls, after-school clubs, and music lessons have kids going here and there, and you find it harder and harder to round up the whole gang for a simple sandwich. These days, it's almost easier to nail a fried egg to a tree than round up teens and their parents for a shared meal.

Hard to believe rounding up the five of us was once as easy as standing in the kitchen, opening a cardboard box, and yelling, "Pizza!"

We used to be able to have dinner together a lot. Of course, we also used to be able to split one Happy Meal between the three kids, and their primary means of transportation was an old red wagon. Believe me, it is much harder to pluck a daughter out of a car pointed in the direction of the mall than to pull her off a Barbie Big Wheel and haul her into the house for dinner. But challenges are no excuse for giving up.

Paul wrote to the Romans,

> We also exult in our tribulations, knowing that tribulation brings about perseverance; and perseverance, proven character; and proven character, hope; and hope does not disappoint, because the love of God has been poured out within our hearts through the Holy Spirit who was given to us. (Romans 5:3-5)

I'd like to paraphrase that:

We don't run scared from frustrations, challenges, or failures with our children. We embrace a bevy of frustrations from potty training to enforcing curfews to outright deceit and disobedience. We don't shy away from the challenges of toddlers, tweeners, adolescents, or even grown children because we know the frustrations and challenges of parenting bring out perseverance; and perseverance, proven character; and proven character, hope; and hope does not disappoint, because the love of God has been poured out within our hearts through the Holy Spirit who was given to us.

Christ is a great role model when it comes to persevering in teaching. He demonstrated tremendous perseverance in ushering those disciples, with their wild mix of temperaments and personalities, across the bridge to maturity.

Jesus taught naturally. He taught continually, conversationally, informally, walking, sitting by the sea, drifting in a boat, through tears, through parables, and through current events. He taught over a skillet of pan-fried fish, and He taught in the face of death. He taught using pictures, stories, and personal examples. You're thinking, *Well, that was fine for Christ; He was deity in the flesh. How does a mere mortal lay a solid faith foundation? How do ordinary moms and dads impart truths about forgiveness, trust, humility, love, commitment, integrity, and honor?*

That question has as many answers as there are people who ask it. God has created the world with a tension between freedom and form. He has made it clear that there is a form to marriage—one husband and one wife, pledging faithfulness to one another—but there is a freedom within that form as to how the man and woman relate to each other. There is an unspoken freedom as to who pays the bills, who picks up the dry cleaning, who makes Sunday brunch, and who calls the plumber. Likewise, God has given us a form for the family—a mother and father who love, nurture, teach God's Word, model God's love, and are careful not to provoke children to anger. Within that form for family lies an expanse of freedom as to how we accomplish those things. God's design is marvelous. It gives us the parameters, then allows us the freedom as creative individuals to express our own personalities within that form.

Fascinated by this idea, for years I've kept my eyes on three families who adhere to the same form of God's ideal for family, yet express themselves differently within the bounds of freedom.

## My Inspiration for Persevering

These families are as different as day and night, yet they share the common bond of success. By success I mean that the parents have fulfilled their God-given responsibilities. By success I *don't* mean that their children have all grown up to become CEOs of major corporations. Nor by success do I mean all their children have grown up and entered full-time ministry. By success I mean that the parents did their level best to nurture faith in their children, and they created home environments where faith was free to flourish.

These parents taught by words and by deeds. They were living examples of faith in action. They put God at the center. They modeled how to be well-adjusted adults and productive members of society. They demonstrated how to take care of their own families as well as how to reach out to others and make an impact on their communities.

One of the families we've kept in sight over the years I have dubbed Classical. They thrive on classical music, classical education, and classical literature. I don't have confirmation, but I suspect their children learned phonics by sounding out the script to Shakespeare's *A Midsummer Night's Dream*. These people had children who instinctively knew to turn the blade of the knife to the *inside* at a table setting. At age two.

Another family is very musical and theatrical—two parts creativity, three parts imagination, and a dash of crazy. I call them the von Trapps. Quotes from Broadway musicals frequently punctuate their conversations, and the mother rarely goes half an hour without singing a little ditty that's racing through her head.

She seems to find it easier to sing a stanza from a Broadway show tune than to make her point in a traditional fashion.

The third family consists of a mom and a dad and four—count 'em, four—boys. Enough said. Well, maybe not quite enough. I've heard the dad say that when the boys were young he never walked into a room without expecting a kid to jump out from behind a door or a sofa or swing down from the ceiling and pounce on his back. I've heard the mom say that some mealtimes became such gross-out sessions she had to leave the table. They had a blast.

While the Classicals, the von Trapps, and the Family with Five Fellas are very different in their compositions and personalities, they each persevered in three things. I call them the three *f*s. These three *f*s, although practiced in a different fashion in each home, reinforced God's idea of family, nurtured an environment where belief was plausible, and artfully wove the natural together with the supernatural.

## The Three Fs

The first *f* is for *firm*. Each one of these families set firm boundaries with their children. When the boundaries are firm, discipline goes to the back burner. By drawing a few, but very strategic, lines in the sand, you say, "These are the rules; abide by them or pay the price." Consequently, you don't have to do a lot of nagging, whining, and counting to three. You know what I mean. "One…two…two and a half…do you hear me? Mommy really means it!"

When the children from these families that we kept in our scope did cross the line, they weren't upbraided in public or chastised in front of strangers. The parents took the child, slipped away, and dealt with the boy or girl in private. By being firm, they didn't spend a lot of time cajoling, pleading, and explaining themselves, which meant they had more time for other things—like having *fun,* which is the second *f.*

Each one of these families, while they had different interests and inclinations, knew how to have a ball. I am confident that if you passed by their open windows you would be far more likely to hear the sounds of laughter than arguing or bickering. They knew how to have fun that didn't depend on a lot of money. They didn't wait for fun until they could afford a trip to Orlando or a week's vacation in the Rockies. They made their own fun with camping trips, board games and popcorn, museums, zoos, forts, puppet shows, bicycle rides, and picnics in the park.

The third *f* they had in common was *no fear.* At least the parents never displayed any fear. They must have been concerned when they launched those kids into middle school, high school, college, and the big, bad world that can eat you alive, but they never let it show. They kept their fears to themselves. However, I have noticed some thick calluses on their knees.

They expressed their fears in prayer. The parents no doubt also shared their fears with each other, but the only thing they revealed to their growing children was a sense of optimism, hope, and high expectations for a bright future.

Even though I have dubbed these parents a success (and they *were* successful in that they were faithful), did they ever have disappointments? Sure they did. Did they experience gut-wrenching heartache and shed a waterfall of tears? Of course. Did they ever wonder how things were going to turn out? Certainly. But the fact that the kids may not have been headed in the direction the parents thought they should be headed never deterred one of them from doing their job as a parent. They stayed the course.

They remained firm, they had fun, and they didn't dump adult fears on small children. Those three *f*s comprise the basics of good parenting. They are principles that stretch back several generations and were at one time widely embraced. I was thinking about the three *f*s and realized I'd seen them somewhere else: in my own home as a little girl.

Through good times and bad, no matter if it was smooth sailing or rough waters, these parents persevered.

## Not Working Solo

Perhaps you're wondering whether you will be able to stay the course.

As a caring and focused parent, you're doing your best to keep up, but you get worn out by mental fatigue. You lie awake at night listening for the garage door to go up. You wonder if you've told your children all the important things you meant to by this age. You wonder if they're trying their hardest at school or if you've been sandbagged. Is a teen naturally thin or does he or she have an eating disorder?

Parents you used to think were on the same page with you are hosting coed sleep-overs. You learn of a spring break trip to a Caribbean island where high-school kids' hotel rooms are stocked with booze—booze purchased by the parents.

You don't like it when the neighbors vote you Most Likely to Be a Neo-Victorian in a Future Life. You are swimming upstream, and you feel it. You hit a few bumps in the road, something comes at you out of left field—something unpleasant, messy, and ugly—and it feels as though a floodgate has opened. Your formerly pleasant, sweet, endearing adolescent has suddenly turned into a sullen, withdrawn recluse. It's as if someone flipped a switch overnight. Some days you feel like throwing in the towel.

There have been days when I have told God that the challenges are too heavy. I have complained that the crises come too close together. I have even told Him I am thinking about quitting, and God has replied, in all caps—God always talks to me in all caps—RESIGNATION REFUSED!

God's Word says we can't quit:

These commandments that I give you today are to be
upon your hearts. Impress them on your children. Talk
about them when you sit at home and when you walk
along the road, when you lie down and when you get
up. (Deuteronomy 6:6-7, NIV)

That is a 24/7 job. Humanly speaking, that's an impossible
job. No human being can do it alone. Which is why we don't
work this job alone. We can rest on the sweet reminder in Isaiah
40:11: "He gently leads those that have young" (NIV).

Sigh. Thank goodness.

God's Word says we don't need to run ourselves frantic
until we crash and burn. We're not flying solo. It may look like
it and feel like it some days, but we're not: "I will be with you;
I will not fail you or forsake you" (Joshua 1:5).

Double sigh. And double thank goodness.

God will be with us. At every stage of parenting, He will be
right there—to comfort, to guide, to offer wisdom, and to offer
hope. He will be with a parent at the washing machine, at the
kitchen sink, in the principal's office, or at the doctor's office.
He will be with you cheering in the bleachers, patting a kid on
the back, or holding a child as he cries on your shoulder.

God will be with a parent who finds vulgar CDs in a school

book bag. He will be there with a parent who discovers pornographic material on a computer screen.

God doesn't just attend award ceremonies and sports recognition dinners. He is always present, ever willing to help in time of trouble. The book of James offers a written guarantee: "If any of you lacks wisdom, let him ask of God, who gives to all generously and without reproach, and it will be given to him" (1:5).

If you understand faith, you know that quitting is not an option. Throwing in the towel when the challenges increase in difficulty and frequency is not a viable possibility. Quitting is never an option in the Christian faith. We run the race to win. Regardless of our own fatigue level, regardless of apparent failure instead of success, regardless of the tears and the heartaches, we don't quit. We run to win.

## Running to Win

To pass on your faith, you need perseverance. Not stubbornness, but perseverance. Stubbornness is an obstinate bullheadedness. It's a pigheadedness that limits itself to a single bellicose parenting strategy that roars, "You'll do it because I said you'll do it!" Perseverance, on the other hand, is quiet and creative. Perseverance requires observation, listening, and a stick-to-itiveness that recognizes the wisdom in searching for a multitude of ways to reach the heart of a child. Looking for new strategies when the old ones don't work, starting over, trying new approaches, regrouping, and taking another run at a problem area can be tiring and frustrating. It can also bring immeasurable pleasure and delight when you see that young person crossing the bridge to adulthood.

Thankfully, God does not expect that, as parents, we produce Billy Grahams, Mother Teresas, John the Baptists, or clones of the apostle Paul. God's expectation is that we persevere. The definition of *perseverance* is "to persist in spite of difficulties."

The word *perseverance* is synonymous with:

- plodding
- patience
- tenacity
- singleness of purpose
- pluck
- stamina
- backbone
- bulldog courage
- grit
- determination

That's exactly what God expects—that we do not quit, cave in, or give up on these kids. He expects that we hang on to them like a dog with a bone. He expects that we stay the course whether the sailing is smooth or the seas are teeming with savage sharks. God expects us to love our kids the way He loves us: with unfailing commitment, a stalwart determination, and an irrational hope.

In late October of 1941, Winston Churchill delivered a brief speech to the school in Harrow, England, that he had attended as a boy. Churchill's remarks were directed to the boys, but he might as well have been addressing their parents. He said, "Never give in, never, never, never, never—in nothing, great or small, large or petty—never give in except to convictions of honour and good sense."

## A Mother Never Quits

MaryRuth Gezon Schans is a marvelous example of a woman who never gave in. At her funeral her son shed light on a marvelous story of his mother's perseverance. MaryRuth and her husband, Marvin, married in 1936. They raised three daughters and one son in a warm and loving home. MaryRuth was a woman most often characterized by kindness, compassion, love, propriety, and poise, as well as her fabulous date cookies that took a full two days to make.

MaryRuth and Marvin's son, David, made a profession of faith at age fourteen. He finished high school and entered college. Then, like a lot of young people, David began drifting away from that faith. "I didn't have much use for Christ anymore," he says, recalling those times.

David drifted through his twenties, his thirties, and his forties. He married, had children, and was a grown man supporting a family of his own. From time to time MaryRuth would gently broach the subject of faith, and David would brush her off. She'd wait awhile, months or maybe years, approach the subject again, and David would brush her off again.

Undaunted by the rebuffs, MaryRuth continued to hope, to pray faithfully for David, and to nudge gently when opportunity presented itself. And if opportunity didn't come to MaryRuth, she went looking for it. When David and his wife, Theresa, moved into a new house in the Chicago area, MaryRuth sent them a Bible. She thought it a perfect housewarming gift.

David opened up the box, saw the Bible inside, and said, "We don't need another Bible. We haven't blown the dust off the one that we have now." He dropped the Bible back into the box, packaged it up, and mailed it back to his mother.

David was fifty-four at the time. MaryRuth was eighty-three. David's children were grown and having children of their own. MaryRuth was a widow now, well into retirement, and getting on in years, her energy beginning to wane. Nobody would have blamed her for feeling completely defeated when she opened the package from David and saw the Bible had been returned.

MaryRuth walked to the phone and dialed David in Illinois.

"David?" she said.

"Mother," he responded.

"David, I know you told me in the note to return the Bible to the store and get the money back. If you had opened the Bible, you would have seen that I'd written in there. I can't take it back."

She wrapped up the Bible and mailed it to him again.

About two years after that exchange, David found his way back to a life of faith. According to David, his hard heart had been softened by the faithful prayers of his mother, his sisters, and the touch of the Holy Spirit. From the time he was a little boy, David had always loved his mother and known that she loved him. But today David has an even deeper love and appreciation for the diligent woman she was. "It was through her prayers over all those years, along with the work of the Holy Spirit, that I have come to know the Lord again."

David has the Bible he and his mother relayed through numerous post offices, and naturally he cherishes it dearly. MaryRuth passed from this life in June of 2002. In November, David and his wife, Theresa, were baptized at the Village Church of Gurnee in Gurnee, Illinois.

## The Secret Is Time

Raising and nurturing children at any stage of the game, attempting to pass on the key components of the Christian faith, requires one of the hottest, most in-demand commodities we are least likely to yield these days—time. We can speak of stretching time, maximizing time, managing time, and stealing time, but in truth, time strikes an unyielding and uncompromising pose.

There are no ways to reconfigure time. There are no divisions to time. There is no such thing as quality time or quantity time. There is only time. Through that steady, constant, even flow of time, we love, nurture, and raise our children. The psalmist knew the importance of time, asking God to "teach us to number our days, that we may present to You a heart of wisdom" (90:12).

Despite helpful books, tapes, seminars, and classes, we all know deep in our hearts that the key ingredient to raising children is time. Plain old ordinary time that comes in limited quantities. Time that can be measured in minutes and seconds. Time that at the end of the day is forever spent and never to be seen again.

In recent years I've grown greedy with time. Not time for myself. Not the "me time" or "mommy time" the women's magazines say we need. The time I yearn for is time with my family.

Maybe it's the ages of our children or the times in which we live, but there's an undercurrent of urgency in the air. A knowledge that the sand is falling to the bottom of the hourglass. Time with children under our roof comes in limited quantities. Which is why, when I turn the calendar to a new month and see blank boxes perched in rows of seven staring back at me, I no longer regard them as opportunities, open spots, or days to fill with scribbled appointments, meetings, and events.

I now guard those squares with a watchful eye. I keep some untouched. I see to it that a fixed number of days, evenings, and weekend afternoons remain empty, free, and clear. Family time. Time to talk about faith, hopes, and dreams of what God may have for our children in the future.

My husband and I are not yielding family time as easily as we used to. We're not giving it up for the school, the soccer field, the movie theater, the television, a thousand extracurricular events, or the mall. Time is a gift, and we're going to spend it wisely and use it intentionally.

Our family has decided to hold some back, to use it to eat together, work together, talk together, pray together, have a few heated discussions together, laugh together—and live life to the hilt.

# Dear Kids

● ● ● ● ● ● ● ● ● ● ● ● ● ● ● ● ● ● ● ● ● ● ● ● ● ●

I n the process of teaching, something almost mystical happens. Ask any teacher, and he or she will verify this is true: The more you teach, the more you learn. It's sort of like a reverse osmosis. The teachers often become the students.

I was thinking about the many things I've learned in the process of teaching my children and was amazed at how long and varied the list is. Then I thought perhaps I should take the opportunity to jot them a formal note of thanks:

*Dear Kids,*

*I've been thinking about the many things I've learned in the process of parenting and teaching you and thought it was high time I said thanks.*

*As infants you taught me flexibility. Had it not been for having babies, I would never have discovered that a woman can make it through a day on only three hours of sleep, half a pack of graham crackers, and a thirty-second shower at 4 P.M.*

*As toddlers you taught me the wonders of the human immune system. Your dirty faces, sticky hands, and runny noses were proof that the human race could survive germ warfare. Spit and a Kleenex may not have earned the Good Housekeeping Seal of Approval, but you taught me the art of improvisation. I also learned I would not die handling locust shells and earthworms and that the picnic was not over simply because someone slapped a frog down on the table next to the carrot sticks.*

*You taught me that a mother who can keep a car on the road when three kids are fighting like cats and dogs in the backseat is a woman who can focus. You also taught me I had the patience to do French braids and decorate a birthday cake with five hundred stars, squeezed one at a time from the tip of a frosting tube.*

*I learned empathy when you struggled in school, humility when you were the kid who drove the soccer ball downfield for the opposing team, and compassion when you had your leg in a cast three times in five years.*

*You taught me to sharpen my reflexes when you learned to ride a bike, and again when you learned to drive a car. I learned to keep a sense of humor when you demanded a pony, and I learned logic when you said, "Why make the bed if I'm just going to mess it up again in a few hours?"*

*You taught me about the speed of time when you announced I should never again buy socks with pictures on them because they were for babies, when you got your first job, and when you appeared for your first date radiating beauty in an elegant dress and upswept hair.*

*Without you I never would have learned a million things to do with an empty cardboard refrigerator box, experienced the joy of draping a bedspread over kitchen chairs, or felt my heart skip a beat as I walked through a parking lot with a growing adolescent who was still willing to slip a hand into mine.*

*Without you I would not have learned the grace and art of fly-fishing, the nuances of bird calls, or the names of the constellations. And without you I would not have experienced the terror of whitewater rafting, the heart palpitations that come from playing basketball in Rollerblades, or the bone-chilling terror of picking up the phone and hearing "There's been a little accident."*

*True, I was often unwilling to learn, but that never stopped a one of you from teaching. They don't teach these kinds of stress survival skills in school. If I had to learn them from someone, I'm glad it was from you.*

*Love, Mom*

To contact the author or to arrange speaking engagements,
send an e-mail to lori@loriborgman.com
or write to Lori Borgman at PO Box 30092
Indianapolis, IN 46230